At Issue

Teen Smoking

Other Books in the At Issue Series:

At Issue

Teen Smoking

Rodger Williams, Book Editor

GREENHAVEN PRESS
A part of Gale, Cengage Learning

GALE
CENGAGE Learning

Detroit • New York • San Francisco • New Haven, Conn • Waterville, Maine • London

Christine Nasso, *Publisher*
Elizabeth Des Chenes, *Managing Editor*

© 2009 Greenhaven Press, a part of Gale, Cengage Learning.

Gale and Greenhaven Press are registered trademarks used herein under license.

For more information, contact:
Greenhaven Press
27500 Drake Rd.
Farmington Hills, MI 48331-3535
Or you can visit our Internet site at gale.cengage.com

For product information and technology assistance, contact us at

Gale Customer Support, 1-800-877-4253
For permission to use material from this text or product, submit all requests online at www.cengage.com/permissions

Further permissions questions can be emailed to permissionrequest@cengage.com

Articles in Greenhaven Press anthologies are often edited for length to meet page require-ments. In addition, original titles of these works are changed to clearly present the main thesis and to explicitly indicate the author's opinion. Every effort is made to ensure that Greenhaven Press accurately reflects the original intent of the authors. Every effort has been made to trace the owners of copyrighted material.

Cover photograph © Images.com/Corbis.

LIBRARY OF CONGRESS CATALOGING-IN-PUBLICATION DATA

Teen smoking / Rodger Williams, book editor.
    p. cm. -- (At issue)
    Includes bibliographical references and index.
    ISBN 978-0-7377-4114-8 (hardcover)
    ISBN 978-0-7377-4115-5 (pbk.)
    1. Teenagers--Tobacco use. 2. Smoking. 3. Tobacco use--Prevention. I. Williams, Rodger.
    HV5745.T444 2009
    362.29'60835--dc22
                                       2008043435

Printed in the United States of America
1 2 3 4 5   15 14 13 12 11

FD083

Contents

Introduction

They are among some of the most popular films of recent years: *Tropic Thunder*; *Hellboy*; *Ocean's Eleven, Twelve,* and *Thirteen*; *Indiana Jones and the Kingdom of the Crystal Skull*; *Anchorman: The Legend of Ron Burgundy*; *Mamma Mia!*; and *Good Night, and Good Luck*. From low-brow comedy to Academy Award–nominated dramas, they all have one thing in common—on-camera smoking. While film industry insiders and others contend that on-camera smoking may be necessary and in some cases integral to these films, others believe that movies like these are influencing young people to take up smoking, and that smoking should be eliminated from films with a teen audience.

In 2005, the journal *Pediatrics* published a study indicating a strong link between smoking in films and an increase in smoking among teenagers. According to the researchers, the prevalence of tobacco use in movies decreased from 1950 until 1990, but rapidly increased thereafter. By the turn of the twenty-first century, the depiction of smoking in movies had returned to pre-1950s levels. The researchers observed that "Beginning in 2002, the total amount of smoking in movies was greater in youth-rated (G/PG/PG-13) films than adult-rated (R) films, significantly increasing adolescent exposure to movie smoking." Because smoking is often perceived by young people as being adult behavior and the negative health impact of smoking is rarely depicted, the researchers believe that tobacco use is being presented in a manner that encourages teens to take up the habit. The authors of the study in *Pediatrics* concluded that one out of every three young people who has begun smoking over the past 15 years has done so as a direct result of the influence of the motion picture industry.

In response to this study, the National Parent Teacher Association, the American Medical Association, the Campaign for Tobacco-Free Kids, as well as numerous other antismoking organizations ran a full-page ad in *Variety* (the entertainment industry's major newspaper) calling on the motion picture industry to give an automatic R rating to any movie depicting smoking. The attorneys general of more than 30 states also called on the industry to run antismoking public service announcements during previews.

But others who have read the study in *Pediatrics* disagree with the notion that smoking in films has a direct impact on teen smoking rates. They point out that the conclusions reached in the "smoking in movies" study are correlative and do not indicate any cause/effect relationship. In other words, they maintain that the study only shows that some teens are choosing to smoke and that smoking is being portrayed in movies more often than in the past; the study proves no connection between the two.

The motion picture industry has also weighed in on the issue of on-screen smoking. They note that smoking can be an integral part of character development and should be allowed in movies without necessitating an R rating. They point to one of the movies mentioned earlier, *Good Night, and Good Luck.* With its depiction of actual TV newsman Edward R. Murrow—a smoker—and the realistic portrayal of smoke-filled newsrooms of 1950s television studios, *Good Night, and Good Luck* was hailed as one of the best movies of 2005 and was nominated for six Academy Awards, including Best Picture, Best Director (George Clooney), and Best Actor (David Strathaim).

Those in the film industry point out that some people and characters *do* smoke, like it or not. Author David Sedaris in his book *When You Are Engulfed in Flames*, writing about having smoking edited out of a reprint of one of his essays, captures view of the creative community:

> The point I argued is that certain people smoke. It's part of what makes them who they are, and though you certainly

don't have to like it, altering someone's character seems a bit harsh, especially when that someone is your mother, and picturing her without a cigarette is unimaginable.

No doubt the debate over how best to address issues related to teen smoking will continue. Some efforts to reduce the number of teen smokers will find adults erring on the side of caution, while others will err on the side of license. The authors of the following articles in *At Issue: Teen Smoking* present differing points of view about this ongoing issue.

1

Teens Are Easily Addicted to Tobacco

Jane E. Brody

Jane E. Brody is a personal health columnist and science news reporter for the New York Times.

A 2007 report indicates that teens can become addicted to tobacco more easily than adults. Teens may experience symptoms of withdrawal within weeks of starting to smoke, underscoring the importance of taking proactive measures to prevent adolescent smoking. Although on the decline for many years, teen smoking has now leveled off and new strategies are needed to combat it.

Dire warning to all adolescents: You can get "hooked from the first cigarette."

That is the headline in the December issue of *The Journal of Family Practice.* In the report that follows, Dr. Joseph R. DiFranza, a family health and community medicine specialist at the University of Massachusetts Medical School in Worcester, states that "very soon after that first cigarette, adolescents can experience a loss of autonomy over tobacco."

Dr. DiFranza, who studies tobacco dependence, described a typical teenage smoker—a 14-year-old girl who smokes only occasionally, about three cigarettes a week. She admitted to having failed at several efforts to quit. Each time she tried, cravings and feelings of irritability drove her back to smoking.

"We have long assumed that kids got addicted because they were smoking 5 or 10 cigarettes a day," Dr. DiFranza said in an interview. "Now we know that they risk addiction after trying a cigarette just once."

He based this conclusion on the findings of a 10-item checklist he and colleagues devised to help people of all ages determine whether they were hooked on nicotine. He reported in the journal:

> "Studies on a cohort of seventh graders found that every symptom on this validated checklist had been experienced by at least one young person within weeks of starting to smoke, sometimes after the first cigarette. These results have been replicated many times."

> "Three New Zealand national surveys involving 25,722 adolescent smokers who used this checklist revealed a loss of autonomy in 25 percent to 30 percent of young people who had smoked their one and only cigarette during the preceding month."

Why Teenagers Are Different

Even occasional teenage smokers can experience the same symptoms of nicotine withdrawal that prompt adult smokers to light up again and again.

The typical adult smoker begins to crave the next cigarette in 45 minutes to an hour after smoking. . . . But kids can be addicted and not need to smoke again for days, even weeks.

Robin J. Mermelstein, director of the Center for Health Behavior Research at the University of Illinois in Chicago and a longtime researcher on smoking behavior, said in an interview that Dr. DiFranza's message was important. But, Dr. Mermelstein added, "the vast majority of teenagers who try one or two cigarettes don't go on to become smokers."

"Some kids experience withdrawal symptoms earlier than others," she continued. "We still need to know how to predict who's going to get hooked."

Dr. DiFranza explained that a phenomenon called "dependence-related tolerance—how long after smoking a cigarette you can go before you need to smoke another one"— was long thought to be the same for adolescents and adults. But recent studies have shown that the brains of adolescents can become tolerant to nicotine after smoking fewer cigarettes than one a day, and it is tolerance that then drives them to smoke more often.

"The typical adult smoker begins to crave the next cigarette in 45 minutes to an hour after smoking," he said. "But kids can be addicted and not need to smoke again for days, even weeks."

Some adult smokers are no different from teenagers. One study found that adults who smoked only a few cigarettes a week found it hard to quit. "They experienced withdrawal symptoms, which some rated as unbearable," Dr. DiFranza reported. "Most of these self-described 'social smokers' were addicted to tobacco."

About one quarter of young people experience a sensation of relaxation the first time they inhale from a cigarette, and this sensation predicts continued smoking.

Decline in Teenage Smoking Has Leveled Off

These findings come at a time when the once steady decline in teenage smoking has leveled off, antismoking ads on television have all but disappeared and smoking in movies has risen to a near all-time high.

"Well over a dozen studies have shown that kids who watch movies with smoking are more likely to smoke," Dr. DiFranza said. "Smoking in movies is more common now than it was in the 1950s and '60s, whereas smoking among adults is half as common now as it was then. Movie producers are not reflecting real life."

Teenage smoking had been declining steadily from peak levels reached in the mid-1990s through 2004, but the rate of decline decelerated during that period, and in 2005 it halted among eighth graders, the bellwether of smoking trends among teenagers. Today, about 13 percent of teenagers smoke at least once a month.

Studies in rats at Duke University revealed how a single cigarette could keep withdrawal symptoms at bay for far longer than the 12 hours it takes for nicotine to be eliminated from the body. The first dose of nicotine increased production of the neurotransmitter noradrenaline in a part of the brain called the hippocampus for at least 30 days after the nicotine was gone. Another Duke study found an increase in nicotine receptors in the brain the day after the animals got their first dose of nicotine.

"The take-home message: It only takes a day for the brain to remodel itself in response to one dose of nicotine," Dr. Di-Franza wrote. "About one quarter of young people experience a sensation of relaxation the first time they inhale from a cigarette, and this sensation predicts continued smoking."

Further evidence of how easily youngsters become addicted to nicotine comes from studies of quit rates among adolescent smokers. In one typical study, 40 percent of adolescents who tried to quit relapsed in one week or less; only 3 percent remained abstinent a year later.

New Strategies Needed

These findings suggest that new, more forceful strategies are needed to combat smoking by youngsters, which typically leads to a lifetime of smoking. More than 90 percent of adult smokers report that they started smoking as adolescents.

Dr. DiFranza maintains that "public health initiatives are most helpful." These include raising the price of cigarettes, a strategy that helped reduce the smoking rate in New York City; a well-enforced nationwide effort to get retailers to stop selling cigarettes to minors; a wider ban on smoking in public places, especially those frequented by teenagers, like restaurants, video game parlors and bowling alleys; mass media campaigns, including broad use by the states of the tobacco industry's payout to sponsor antismoking commercials; and pressure on the movie industry to make films smoke-free.

He urged parents, including those who smoke themselves, to emphasize to their children that "it's a huge mistake to start smoking. If they never start, they'll never have to worry about quitting."

2

Teen Smoking Rates Are at a Standstill

Rob Stein

Rob Stein is a national science reporter who focuses on health and medicine for the Washington Post.

Rates of teen smoking declined between 1997 and 2003, but have now stalled. Antismoking organizations are asking politicians to renew efforts to reduce tobacco use and calling for new public health campaigns. The organizations blame the plateau on increased marketing by tobacco companies, though these companies do sponsor programs discouraging teen smoking.

The campaign to reduce teenagers' smoking has stalled, new federal data show, dismaying federal health officials and anti-smoking advocates who said that one of the nation's most important public health priorities is faltering.

Decline in Teen Smoking Levels Stalled

Smoking by teenagers fell sharply and steadily between 1997 and 2003, but the latest data from a large federal survey tracking smoking and other risky behaviors among young people found the proportion of teens who smoke leveled off between 2003 and 2007.

"This is the most dramatic indication that the great progress we're making has stalled," said Terry Pechacek of the federal Centers for Disease Control and Prevention in Atlanta, which released the new data last week. "This has very negative long-term implications."

The lack of greater progress in recent years is a clear warning to elected officials to resist complacency and redouble efforts to reduce tobacco use.

Anti-smoking advocates agreed.

"More progress must be made to ensure youngsters at these critical age levels continue to turn away from smoking," Cheryl Healton of the American Legacy Foundation, a Washington-based anti-smoking group, said in a statement.

"The lack of greater progress in recent years is a clear warning to elected officials to resist complacency and redouble efforts to reduce tobacco use. We know how to win the fight against tobacco use, but we will not win it—and our progress could even reverse—without the political leadership to implement proven solutions," Matthew L. Myers of the Campaign for Tobacco-Free Kids, a Washington advocacy group, said in a statement.

The data released last week come from the Youth Risk Behavior Survey, a nationally representative survey that the federal government conducts of students in grades 9 through 12 every two years to track a variety of risk behaviors, including drug, alcohol and tobacco use.

The proportion of students who smoke soared from 27.5 percent in 1991 to 36.4 percent in 1997 but then began to fall, hitting 21.9 percent in 2003. The 2005 survey, however, showed the rate had crept up to 23 percent. Because that change was not statistically significant, officials were waiting for the 2007 figures to determine whether the downward trend had actually stalled.

The 2007 figure is slightly lower at 20 percent, but again, the figure is not statistically significant.

"We had a dramatic increase from 1991 to 1997 and then a reversal of that problematic upward trend from 1997 to 2003. In 2005 it was not declining, but we hoped that was a short-term bump," Pechacek said. "We're always cautious about making long-term implications from one data point. We were hoping that we would be back on track this year. But we're not."

One in five kids is still smoking.

While the survey did show continued declines in some groups, most notably African American girls, the overall downward trend stalled.

Why Teen Smoking Rates Are Not Declining

"There have been fluctuations between subgroups, but the bottom line is we are not on the decline anymore. We are confident that is a scientifically defined fact," Pechacek said.

"One in five kids is still smoking. Another generation is continuing on with a high rate of tobacco use into adulthood where the industry can prey on them and maintain this epidemic into another generation," he said. "This is a major public health concern."

Pechacek blamed the trend in part on cuts on anti-smoking campaigns by states that had been funded by a nationwide 1998 settlement of a class-action lawsuit against the tobacco industry.

"Many large states had very active campaigns that went off the air," he said, citing Massachusetts, Florida and Mississippi as examples of states that had cut their programs.

At the same time, cigarette companies have continued to increase their spending on promotional activities, including heavily advertising brands that teenagers are most likely to smoke, working to feature smoking in movies and videos and offering pricing incentives that offset increases in cigarette prices.

"The tobacco industry never stopped promoting its products," Pechacek said. "They have increased their effort and maintained a very active effort to promote tobacco while prevention efforts have lost funding."

Bill Phelps, a spokesman for Altria Group, the parent company of Philip Morris USA, said his company has a variety of programs aimed at discouraging teen smoking, including punishing stores found selling cigarettes to children.

"We believe kids should not use tobacco," Phelps said. "We have a pretty significant youth smoking prevention program."

3

Teen Smoking Rates Are on the Decline

Harvard Health Publications Group

Harvard Health Publications is a division of the Harvard Medical School that works to bring the public practical, authoritative health information through newsletters, books, and the Internet.

Smoking, as well as other addictive behaviors, continues a decline begun in the 1990s, according to a study conducted by the University of Michigan. Rates went down most dramatically among younger teenagers; declines were smaller among high school students. Parents, educators, and medical professionals need to work together in identifying addictive behaviors and developing strategies to assist teens in avoiding all kinds of addictions.

Youth smoking and drug abuse declined again this year, concludes a federal study that also found marked progress over the last decade in persuading teens to avoid cigarettes and illicit substances.

The smoking rate among younger teens is half what it was in the mid-1990s, and drug use by that group is down by one-third, says the University of Michigan study, done for the National Institute on Drug Abuse and released . . . [August 2006]. Less dramatic strides have been made among older teens.

Altogether, gains in 2004 over 2003 were modest. Researchers were bothered by increases in the use of inhalants such as glue, aerosols and the pain-control narcotic OxyContin. Use of most other drugs declined or held steady.

When smoking makes a teen less attractive to the great majority of the opposite sex, as now appears to be the case, one of the long-imagined benefits for adolescent smoking is seriously undercut.

This was the eighth consecutive year that smoking rates among surveyed teens dropped, a turnaround that began in 1996 among students in grades eight and 10 and a year later among 12th-graders.

"We know that young people have come to see cigarette smoking as more dangerous, while they also have become less accepting of cigarette use, and these changes continued into 2004," said Lloyd Johnston, lead researcher for the Monitoring the Future study.

Researchers credited higher cigarette prices, tighter marketing practices, anti-smoking ads and withdrawal of the Joe Camel logo among the reasons smoking has fallen out of favor with more teens. Close to three-quarters of surveyed 12th-graders now say they'd rather not date a smoker, up from close to one-third in 1977.

"When smoking makes a teen less attractive to the great majority of the opposite sex, as now appears to be the case, one of the long-imagined benefits for adolescent smoking is seriously undercut," Johnston said.

Encouraging Signs of Tobacco Decline

Overall, the percentage of eighth-graders who had ever tried cigarettes declined to 28 percent this year [2006] down half a percentage point from 2003 and from a peak of 49 percent in 1996.

About 41 percent of 10th-graders had tried cigarettes, down 1 percentage point from a year earlier and from 61 percent in 1996.

And 53 percent of seniors had smoked at least once in their lives, down 1 percentage point from 2003 and from more than 65 percent in 1997.

Even so, cigarette use has hardly been stamped out among youth. The study reported that 25 percent of 12th-graders said they had smoked within 30 days of being surveyed, as did 16 percent of 10th-graders and 9 percent of eighth-graders.

The study also found that progress in discouraging teen drinking in recent years held steady for the lower grades in 2004. Researchers said it would take another year to know whether a small increase indicated in drinking by seniors was real or a statistical blip.

They reported a gradual decline in drug use this year over last. Eighth-graders have been less apt to use drugs for eight years running while drug use among seniors has declined for three years.

The survey found 15 percent of eighth-graders, 31 percent of 10th-graders and 39 percent of 12th-graders had used drugs in the previous year—down 1 percentage point or less from the year before.

Inhalants emerged as a particular concern; their use went up in all three grades last year and again, marginally, in 2004.

Within that drug group, researchers noted the apparent growing popularity of OxyContin, which up to 5 percent of seniors and smaller percentages of younger teens reported having tried in the last year. By contrast, 1 percent or less of teens had tried heroin in a year.

OxyContin is a powerful and potentially addictive synthetic narcotic.

The study questioned 50,000 students in about 400 schools nationwide as part of a series that began three decades ago with high school seniors. Surveys of eighth-graders and 10th-graders were added in 1991.

Tobacco Use Is Part of a Bigger Issue

Although parents may find it hard to believe that their school-aged children might take a drink of alcohol or use other drugs, it is true! Many children try smoking cigarettes, drinking alcohol, or trying other drugs at very young ages. Fortunately, the results of this most recent study that questioned 50,000 students in about 400 schools nationwide are promising.

Part of a series that began 30 years ago with high school seniors (eighth-graders and 10th-graders were added in 1991), this survey showed that youth smoking and drug abuse went down again last year. The smoking rate among younger teens has been cut in half compared with the mid-1990s; drug use by this same group has dropped by one-third. While the size of the drop among older teens may not have been as large, the results were still important. Smoking appears not to be as attractive as it used to be. For example, close to three-quarters of surveyed 12th-graders now say they'd rather not date a smoker, almost doubled from 1977. . . .

While the use of most drugs did go down or at least stayed the same, the use of inhalants did not. Their use actually went up in all three grades last year and slightly up again this year. Sadly, OxyContin, a powerful and potentially addictive narcotic, seems to be gaining popularity as well. . . .

Addiction Issues Must Be Addressed Early

It is most important that you talk with your child today about the dangers of alcohol and drug use! You can help your child learn the real truth about alcohol and drug use. Starting at a young age, use any and every opportunity to talk with your child about drugs and alcohol. In one survey of fourth graders, 2 out of 3 said that they wished their parents would talk more with them about drugs.

Researchers and health professionals must be informed and also looking for new things that our youth may experiment with, use, and abuse.

Do not worry that you will "put ideas" into your child's head. If you do not talk with your child, he will learn about drugs and alcohol from the world around him. He would much rather learn from you, his favorite, most-trusted, and best teacher. The Partnership for a Drug-Free America, on behalf of the United States Department of Education, offers advice for teaching your child about drugs. You can also ask your child's doctor what ways s/he thinks work well.

All parents need to know about inhalants (gases and vapors from common household products) that are inhaled on purpose. Inhalants are poisonous gases and vapors that are released into the air from aerosol (spray) cans, fuels, solvents, and solvent-based products. Examples include cooking spray, disinfectants, felt-tip markers, furniture polish and wax, air fresheners, spray deodorants, hair spray, nail polish removers, butane (found in cigarette lighters), gasoline, glues (like model airplane glue and contact cement), paints, paint thinners, and spray paints. These dangerous poisons can cause serious injury throughout the body, and even death, when inhaled. Parents must teach their children about the dangers of inhalants at early ages. These appear to be popular because they can be found quite readily throughout the house and therefore are easy to get. In addition, many adults do not even know about inhalants and may not suspect they are being abused.

Researchers and health professionals must be informed and also looking for new things that our youth may experiment with, use, and abuse. Studies like this one need to be done regularly and the results shared with all of us. The government will also continue to look for the best ways to eliminate all smoking, drinking of alcohol, and use of drugs by children.

Behavioral scientists will continue to explore how best to get these very important messages across to children of all ages. Adults are role models for children, so all of us must help all children at young ages to learn between good and bad behaviors, using approaches that match a child's level of development and understanding.

Smoking Among Teen Girls Is Still a Problem

Marta De Borba-Silva

Marta De Borba-Silva is a doctoral student in health education and promotion at the Loma Linda University School of Public Health in California.

Teen girls are beginning to smoke at a greater rate than teen boys. Reasons for this trend may include the particular pressures on young women during adolescence—especially that of body image. There is a misguided belief that smoking will help teens remain thin. Historically, boys have not been under the same pressures about their bodies as young women. Open communication between teen girls and the adults in their lives is the key to reducing the number of young women who smoke.

Smoking will eventually kill more teens than all other combined methods of death. Large-scale studies have firmly established that one in two life-long smokers dies from smoking, half while in middle age. With each cigarette smoked, seven minutes of life is lost. Smoking diseases such as lung cancer with low cure rates tend to be very painful ways to die. So, why are so many teenage girls—as compared to teenage boys—taking up a deadly habit more addictive than heroin? The answers can be found by examining the marketing practices of the tobacco industry, today's American culture, and most importantly, the role of parents.

Marta De Borba-Silva, "The Alarming Trend of Teen Girl Smoking," *Pediatrics for Parents*, August 2007. Copyright © 2007 Pediatrics for Parents, Inc. Reproduced by permission. www.pedsforparents.com.

Among US adults who have ever smoked daily, 82% tried their first cigarette before age 18, and 53% became daily smokers before 18. According to the recently released National Survey on Drug Use and Health, approximately 3,500 American youths aged 12 to 17 try their first cigarette each day. The good news is this is down about 20%, from 4,400 per day, in 2000, but the bad news is the number of girls smoking compared to boys is increasing. In 2004, 730,000 girls began smoking as compared to 565,000 boys.

A study of adolescent never-smokers ... determined that tobacco marketing is a stronger influence in encouraging teens to smoke than exposure to peer, family smokers or demographic variables.

The World Health Organization (WHO)/Centers for Disease Control and Prevention (CDC) Global Youth Tobacco Survey of 2000 found for the first time that female students in the US were smoking at the same rate as male students. In all other regions of the world, male youth continued to out-smoke females. The 2002 CDC Youth Tobacco Study found an 18% decrease in smoking from 2000 among 9th through 12th graders, but the decrease among middle school students, grades six to eight, was not statistically significant. Smoking prevalence decreased just 0.2% for middle school girls while decreasing 1.5% among boys. Smoking tends to be more popular among white teen girls. The CDC found in 1999 that 40% of white high school females were current smokers compared to 32% of Latino and 19% of African-American high school females.

Tobacco companies deny marketing to youth, but a look at the numbers says otherwise. In order to maintain current market size and profits, tobacco manufacturers must recruit approximately 4,000 new smokers each day to replace the 1,100 smokers who die and the 3,000 smokers who quit.

The Global Youth Tobacco Survey Collaborating Group, in their report Difference in Worldwide Tobacco Use by Gender, found that cigarette promotion and marketing influences adolescent smoking behavior to a far greater extent than adult behavior. A study of adolescent never-smokers also determined that tobacco marketing is a stronger influence in encouraging teens to smoke than exposure to peer, family smokers or demographic variables.

Advertising Taps into the Teen Market

Big Tobacco is number two, just behind the automotive industry, for advertising expenditures in the US. Since 1997, tobacco marketing budgets have doubled, with over $12 billion currently spent each year. Since tobacco advertising is not allowed on television, radio, or billboards, 80% of this $12 billion yearly budget is spent on retail promotional marketing—at the 7-11s, Circle Ks, and AM PMs of America—where teens easily congregate and often find no carding required to purchase cigarettes. A study done in a town east of San Francisco found that compared to other stores in the same community, stores where adolescents shopped frequently had three times more marketing materials for Marlboro, Camel, and Newport, the three most popular brands smoked by American youth. Surveys of established adolescent smokers have found that retail stores are their primary source for tobacco. The other 20% of Big Tobacco's marketing budget is spent on event sponsorship and magazine advertising. In 2002, a California court found RJR Nabisco guilty of targeting youth through the selective placement of ads in magazines with high youth readership. Women's magazines' dependence on revenue from tobacco advertising has stifled coverage of the health consequences of smoking and has muted criticism of the tobacco industry.

Adolescents, still in the process of discovering who they are and who they aspire to be, learn much about the world and about smoking by watching celebrity behavior in the media. Actresses in movies tend to be beautiful, affluent and powerful, smoking in the context of romance, to appear tough, or to relieve stress—all situations adolescents might aspire to. One study that examined four decades of movies found the number of smoking scenes in 1990s movies to be at 1960s levels, before we knew the dangers of tobacco. Another study found that 89% of the top 200 movie rentals in 1996 and 1997 had scenes with tobacco. Fifth graders with high exposure to movie smoking had higher smoking rates than eighth graders with low exposure, even after controlling for sixteen other factors. Another study found that adolescents in the highest quartile of exposure to movie smoking were 2.71 times more likely to initiate smoking than those in the lowest quartile. Children with parental restrictions on R-rated movies had substantially lower risk for smoking.

Cigarette ads in women's magazines certainly sell the message that smoking helps with weight control—thin as rail models and even the name "Virginia Slims."

Why Girls Smoke

According to the 2001 Surgeon General's report on women and smoking, girls who start smoking are more likely to have parents or friends who smoke and have stronger attachments to peers than family. They also perceive smoking prevalence to be higher than it is, tend to be rebellious, have weaker commitments to school or religion, have less knowledge of the adverse consequences and addictiveness of smoking, and believe it can control weight and negative moods. They also tend to have positive images of smokers.

Adolescence is a difficult time, but more so for girls than boys. Girls become sensitive and their self-confidence goes down; they may struggle with insecurity and depression—cliques, boys, looks, and weight. Our culture does not have such rigid standards of looks and weight and being "the right way" for boys. Every day, however, girls are bombarded with unrealistic images of "the ideal female" on magazine covers, television, and in the movies—our whole cult of celebrity. Partly because of hormonal changes, one in four adolescent girls suffers from depression, 50% higher than boys. Smoking becomes a way to mask this adolescent angst behind a protective wall of conformity, a solution to their anxieties. Girls preoccupied with their weight are more likely to take up smoking. Girls who diet daily are twice as likely as girls who diet less often to have tried smoking. And, compared with girls who report not dieting, those dieting more than twice a week have four times the odds of becoming smokers. Cigarette ads in women's magazines certainly sell the message that smoking helps with weight control—thin as rail models and even the name "Virginia Slims."

For unknown reasons, girls seem to develop symptoms of nicotine addiction faster than boys, and women appear to be more susceptible to tobacco's carcinogenic effects. Dose-response odds ratios were 1.2- to 1.7-fold higher in women compared to men when looking at lung cancer susceptibility in one study. In 1987, lung cancer surpassed breast cancer as the leading cause of cancer death among women. In 1950, lung cancer accounted for only 3% of all female cancer deaths while in 2000 it was 25%. Current smoking is also associated with a higher risk for myocardial infarction in women compared to men, especially in women younger than 45.

Addressing the Issue Head-On

Parents are the most powerful antidote to the tobacco marketing practices and cultural pressures placed on today's American teen girls. Parents who consistently disapprove of tobacco, are positively engaged in their daughters' lives and have established rules and standards of behaviors have one-fourth the risk of their teens abusing substances than parents who are not as attuned to, and involved in, their daughters' lives. The National Center on Addiction and Substance Abuse (CASA) has consistently found that the more often teens have dinner with their parents, the less likely they are to smoke, drink or use drugs.

Just as Big Tobacco has their "Four As" for marketing cigarettes:

- Aspirational—making cigarettes desirable and fashionable

- Acceptable—making cigarettes socially and culturally acceptable

- Accessible—making cigarettes available and affordable

- Addictive—keeping smokers paying for cigarettes for long term

Parents have the "Four Ms" to raise healthy, tobacco-free daughters:

- Maximize time together to build a strong bond

- Model coping skills to manage stress and pressure

- Motivate their daughters' self-confidence by recognizing their strengths, skills, and interests

- Monitor their daughters' activities and behaviors with love and limits

Information on how to incorporate these four Ms into a healthy family life can be found at www.theantidrug.com, and additional facts on why girls are at increased risk for smoking and other risky behaviors at www.freevibe.com. . . . the "five As" clinical approach to smoking cessation can help [girls that already smoke]:

- Ask about her tobacco use

- Advise her to stop

- Assess her willingness to quit

- Assist her in formulating a quit plan

- Arrange for further advice and encouragement

The website www.whyquit.com contains a wealth of prevention and cessation resources.

5

Smokeless Tobacco Use Is Increasing Among Teens

Jessica Cohn

Jessica Cohn is a contributor for Weekly Reader Publications.

While the message that smoking tobacco is dangerous to one's health is just about common knowledge among people of all ages, the dangers of smokeless tobacco are not so. Only 40 percent of teens are aware of the health risks of smokeless tobacco— cancers of the mouth, tongue, and esophagus being among them. With its immediate and strong high coupled with the ignorance of its dangers, smokeless tobacco use is increasing among teens.

Rob Leeret started to chew tobacco at 14. "In middle school, it was just out there, and everybody was trying it," says Leeret, now 36. "I remember basically making myself sick a couple of times."

Leeret and his friends were warned about drug use but not about smokeless tobacco (ST). So he didn't think much about possible health effects, and neither do many teens today. Despite some serious consequences, the number of teens overall using ST is rising among both sexes. The Centers for Disease Control and Prevention identifies 11 percent of high school males and 2 percent of females as ST users.

Facts of the Matter

You've heard that smoking kills people. With ST, there's no smoke, which leads to confusion about its health effects. The product is packaged in wads or blocks or is powdered. Users stick some between the upper lip, the lower lip, and the cheek and gum—or they chew it. But ST isn't bubble gum. The effect is very direct: Users feel a short high followed by a long low as the chemicals work through their systems.

A newer product called snus (rhymes with juice) looks like a small tea bag. Some cancer-causing chemicals have been removed, so it's marketed as a safer product than cigarettes and as a way to help smokers quit. But use of all forms of tobacco raises heart attack risk, according to a study in the *Lancet* medical journal. "Tobacco is tobacco is tobacco," says Dr. Greg Connolly, director of the Tobacco Control Research Program at Harvard University in Boston. "It's not a healthy thing."

That's an understatement. Smokeless tobacco contains thousands of chemicals, including the poison arsenic and polonium-210, a nuclear waste. It's not surprising, then, that ST has scary health effects. Tobacco chemicals cause 75 percent of cancers of the mouth, tongue, lips, and throat, according to the American Dental Association. Cancer from ST can also affect the esophagus, stomach lining, and urinary bladder.

There are two studies indicating that young people who [use] smokeless tobacco are more likely to go on to smoke tobacco.

Despite the dangers, ST warnings are few, and the lack of public education shows. About 77 percent of teens think smoking is harmful. But only 40 percent know ST is loaded with trouble, according to the U.S. surgeon general.

Perhaps that helps explain why ST use is growing. A survey of Indiana students last year revealed that, though fewer used alcohol, marijuana, and other drugs and a decrease in smoking remained steady, more teens were using ST. Nationwide, about 15 percent of 10th graders and 18 percent of 12th graders have used ST at least once, according to the Monitoring the Future study, with nearly a 1 percent increase in each grade from 2004 to 2005.

Personal Message

Gruen Von Behrens, 29, has a personal mission. He used ST as a teen in Illinois. He learned the hard way that "smokeless does not mean harmless," as he tells CH [*Current Health*].

Von Behrens started using ST at age 13. At 17, he found a white spot in his mouth. Within nine months, cancer had eaten his tongue. He then lost his jawbone. His voice became hard to understand. Von Behrens tells his story to students as a warning. "This is a decision I made [16] years ago, and it has affected my whole life," he says. "There are certain jobs that I [can't] get. Some people don't accept me because of the way I talk."

Chew on This!

Like many unhealthy habits, ST use often begins in the teen years. Of the roughly 13 million Americans who use ST, one-third are under age 21. More than half started before age 13.

Experimentation with ST can quickly turn into an all-consuming habit. With repeated use, more ST is necessary to deliver what users felt initially; longtime users end up buying brands with more nicotine. A can of tobacco contains as much nicotine as 60 cigarettes, and Leeret was up to two cans a day. (That's $10 daily!)

Plus he was smoking cigarettes. That's not a rarity, according to tobacco experts. "There are two studies indicating that young people who [use] smokeless tobacco are more likely to go on to smoke tobacco," says Connolly.

Last year, Leeret's 12-year-old daughter asked for three things for her birthday: a sleep-over, a video game, and for her dad to quit tobacco. She didn't have to tell him that he should. As nursing director at a Denver medical center, Leeret knew the medical reasons why his heart was beating irregularly. He knew why skin shed off his gums each morning.

Leeret says everyone should be taught that ST is "like heroin, [methamphetamine], crack. You do it and get hooked. You'll have to go through some kind of recovery to get off it."

The first three days off ST were the hardest, he says. A week later, Leeret was still uncomfortable but doing his best. "The thing is, you're thinking of chew as a safe alternative to cigarettes, but it's just not true," says Leeret.

Signs of Oral Cancer

- sore or an irritation that bleeds easily and won't heal

- color changes in mouth, such as white spots or red bumps

- pain, tenderness, or numbness in the mouth or on the lips

- lump or a rough, crusty area

- change in how your teeth fit together with your mouth closed

6

Cigar Use Is Increasing Among Teens

David Graham

David Graham is a columnist with the Toronto Star.

Smoking cigars has become one of the newest trends among young smokers. It is no mistake that teens are drawn to smoking cigars because they are now flavored, much like candy. And, often sold individually and inexpensively, they can be easier on the wallet than a pack of cigarettes. The flavoring and packaging of these cigars might distract some from their dangers; one cigar can pack the tobacco content of an entire pack of cigarettes. Coupled with the fact that most cigar smokers also smoke cigarettes on a regular basis, the health of young people is severely at risk. Doing away with counter displays of these cigars in convenience stores may help curtail their use. However, attention also needs to be given to other avenues that teens use to obtain their tobacco—including the Internet.

Among the Gummi Bears and Snickers bars, lottery tickets and smokes, sit displays brimming with the latest childhood treat.

In brightly lit convenience stores filled with colourful candies and sugary sweets, flavoured cigars are discreetly presented as inexpensive and cool alternatives to cigarettes.

Sometimes they're relegated to the "power wall" of other tobacco products looming behind the cashier. But just as often

David Graham, "Smoke and Mirrors," *The Toronto Star*. March 31, 2006, p. D01. Copyright © 2006 Toronto Star Newspapers, Ltd. Reproduced by permission of Torstar Syndication Services.

they hover precariously close to the candy counter, within reach of the pint-sized impulse buyer.

To be honest, I know they're dangerous but I'm not concerned. I don't inhale.

Chocolate and berry flavoured, honey drenched and sugar-tipped, these miniature cigars smell and taste delicious. And health experts worry a whole generation of kids yearning for the forbidden symbols of adulthood may be under the false impression these candied killers in pretty packages with such names as Prime Time, Backwoods and Pinto are less harmful than cigarettes.

Andrew, a 15-year-old Grade 10 student from Oakville swears by the strawberry, raspberry and mint chocolate flavoured Prime Time cigars that he started smoking five months ago. "They look so tasty," he says of the shiny, colourful wrapper.

"They are sold in singles. They are small and they're not expensive," he says. Most products sell for around $1, sometimes less.

What's more, Andrew is convinced he has what it takes to control the addictive nature of nicotine. "To be honest I know they're dangerous but I'm not concerned. I don't inhale," says the teen, who also smokes about a pack of cigarettes a week. He admits he's "probably addicted" but insists that, in time, he'll quit.

"I'm only planning to smoke for one to five years so it's not going to have a huge effect on my life," he says.

Teens smoking cigars—it's a growing concern in the United States, where mainstream media are starting to report on the alarming trend.

In [Canada] it's not clear exactly how many teens are picking up the habit, but here's the deal: They're everywhere and they're not hard to get.

How Teens Get Their Cigars

In Canada, cigars are governed by the same laws that control the sale of cigarettes. Andrew, well under the legal age of 19, has to be creative when exercising his purchasing power. Sometimes he's emboldened and simply asks clerks at corner stores, hoping he won't get carded. If that doesn't work he employs the "shoulder tapping" method, asking a stranger to make the purchase for him. A third alternative involves the recruitment of a friend's older sibling.

During a break from school this week [March 2006] we asked two non-smoking teenaged girls, 14 and 17, to try their luck buying both cigarettes and flavoured cigars in 10 different Toronto corner stores. The 17-year-old was successful at three locations and scored two cigar products and a package of cigarettes. The 15-year-old was only successful once for cigarettes and once for cigars.

Cynthia Callard, executive director of Physicians for a Smoke-Free Canada, is incensed that these products are allowed on the market. On its website, her organization notes that cigar smoking is on the rise in Canada, citing figures from a 2000 edition of the trade magazine *Tobacco Journal International* that showed sales increased by 13 per cent in each of the five previous years to 228 million units in 1999. Most of that business was controlled by the Old Port Cigar Co., which was owned by Imperial Tobacco until it was sold in 2000 to a Danish company "at a time of robust sales," according to the trade magazine *Smokeshop*. At the time Imperial made five million cigars and 120 million cigarillos.

Callard is concerned that the federal regulatory system allows tobacco companies to "introduce whatever they like" because "there are no conditions required to obtain a licence" to make cigars and worse, "there is no consistency surrounding the use of health warning labels."

Andre Blais, marketing manager of Old Port Cigar Co., says he is reluctant to talk to mainstream media because Canadian legislation prohibits his company from engaging in any advertising or public relations activities related to the sale of tobacco products. He says he is concerned his comments could be misconstrued as an attempt to promote the company's Pinto cigarillos, which have been on the market for six months.

More importantly, Blais explains that health warnings for the Pinto product, sold as singles, are located on the shipping package, which the end consumer rarely sees.

One large cigar can expose the smoker to the same amount of nicotine found in a whole pack of cigarettes.

To its credit, a Backwoods brand of Mild 'n Natural Cigars—honey/berry flavoured—carries a warning: "Where There's Smoke There's Poison" and "Tobacco smoke contains more than 50 cancer-causing agents." A warning printed on the wrapper of a Prime Time chocolate mint flavoured cigarillo acknowledges it may cause cancer and birth defects or other reproductive harm.

There's no question cigars have been given a younger, trendier image. They have been connected with entertainers such as Jay-Z and sports personalities like Michael Jordan. Jay-Z extolled the virtues of cigars in *USA Today*: "A cigar gives you an air of invincibility."

The Cigar Market Expands

While adults have been the target market for cigars, which are usually part of the luxury category that includes fine wines, champagne and single malt scotches, now they are attracting the attention of kids. The flavoured cigar category has expanded from Courvoisier, Kahlua or Amaretto to strawberry, raspberry and chocolate. Sometimes they are sugar-tipped to bevel the sharp tobacco taste.

Health Canada reports that cigar smoking carries all the same risks as cigarette smoking, while a report published in the *Journal of the American Medical Association* in 2000 said smoking one large cigar can expose the smoker to the same amount of nicotine found in a whole pack of cigarettes. And just like cigarettes, cigars cause cancers of the lung and upper digestive tract.

As the tobacco industry struggles to stay alive in the wake of plummeting cigarette sales, it appears to be hanging at least some hope for survival on these tiny tasty cigars.

Tobacco manufacturers and retailers say they do not market these products to underaged consumers. But research by the antismoking lobby reveals the tobacco industry is fully aware its future lies in its ability to hook people when they're young.

Rob Cunningham, a senior policy analyst with the Canadian Cancer Society, says he doesn't know of any study that supports the connection between flavoured cigarillos and teenagers.

"We don't have data but it's clearly a concern," he says. "Regardless of their intent, they are still attracting underage children to their product. There's no doubt that the tobacco industry on the whole is a declining market. And all new smokers begin in their teens or pre-teens."

Amanda Sandford, research manager for the London-based Action on Smoking and Health, has good reason to mistrust the intentions of the tobacco industry. Her organization published a 1999 brochure, Tobacco Explained, that featured a chapter on marketing to children, a compendium of "notes" lifted from internal documents from industry players.

The documents reveal that tobacco companies have looked at potential customers as young as 5. "As one executive says, 'They got lips, we want them,'" the document reads. It was followed up recently with another report called "Trust Us: We're The Tobacco Industry."

While the study deals primarily with advertising and marketing strategies that existed before new laws banned such ads, the study underscores the tobacco industry's dilemma: How to get teens on board, "hooked," without drawing attention to its motives. The documents could have served as a template for the black comedy *Thank You For Smoking*, which spoofs the pro-smoking lobby. The film opened in Toronto last week.

"The tobacco industry has always denied that they targeted children," says Sandford. But as the British brochure reveals, there's no better way to capture the attention of teens than by insisting the product is for adults only.

These are desperate times for the tobacco industry as, each year, legislation hobbles its efforts to increase business.

Making It Tougher for Teens to Get Cigars

Cunningham is thrilled with tough new Ontario legislation that comes into effect this May 31 [2006]. It's all part of the Smoke-Free Ontario Act, which will prohibit the countertop displays of all tobacco products. And it gets tougher. On May 31, 2008, all displays of all tobacco products will be banned. The "power walls" filled with every brand imaginable that stand behind clerks in convenience stores will no longer exist.

The next frontier may be the Internet, but even there manufacturers and retailers insist they are not targeting youth.

The website for Pennsylvania-based Turner Business Services Cigars, the distributor for Cojimar and Prime Time, insists the company abides by the rules but acknowledges there are rogue online tobacco retailers.

"The Internet has become a vast world of retailers who sell cigarillos and other tobacco online without knowing all the regulations or choose not to comply with the laws for tobacco because they feel they will not get caught ... We make every effort to ensure full compliance and disclose that fact to you because we would never want one of our customers to be involved in an underage tobacco investigation. Our business was established in 1999 with a single website and today, over 60 websites strong, we are proud to say that we are here to stay."

7

Parents Can Influence Teens Not to Smoke

Katy Abel

Katy Abel is a writer for Family Education Network.

Parents are not powerless when they discover that their teenager has taken up smoking. Rather than feeling as though they must simply accept a situation that they may not like, parents can use their influence to discourage smoking. Parental attitudes, open lines of communication, and strong punishment for smoking can all help smoking teens to kick the habit and encourage nonsmoking teens never to begin.

Sixteen-year-old Haley A.'s New Year's resolution is to not criticize other people. As admirable as that goal may be, Haley's mother wishes her daughter had made another resolve: to quit smoking. But the teen is indifferent to the idea. She enjoys smoking, and at five or six cigarettes a day, does not believe she is addicted to nicotine.

"I think if I had something to motivate me, I could stop really easily," Haley says. "For me, it's a boredom thing. Whenever I'm bored, it's something to do."

The honor roll student who says she's the only smoker in her circle of friends is bucking a national trend. Monitoring the Future, a new survey released by the U.S. Department of Health and Human Services and the University of Michigan's Institute for Social Research, shows teen smoking in grades 8,

10, and 12 is declining "at a vigorous pace." This is a direct contrast to the early 1990s, when researchers saw a dramatic increase in the number of teens lighting up. Among eighth-graders, smoking rates fell from 21 percent in 1996 to 12 percent in 2001; and among tenth-graders, from 30 percent to 21 percent. Among high-school seniors, smoking rates dropped from 37 percent in 1997 to 30 percent in 2001.

Researchers say that Hispanic parents, even if they smoke themselves, are less likely to allow teens to smoke in the house.

The study attributed the decreases to the demise of the Joe Camel ad campaign, the increase in anti-smoking ads, and the jump in cigarette prices in most states.

"Young people are price-sensitive in their use of cigarettes," says the study's principal investigator, Dr. Lloyd D. Johnston of the University of Michigan. "When the price goes up, it is less likely that (kids) will proceed to greater use."

Parents, Not Just Media, Need to Send Signals

What about the influence of parents? While the latest survey didn't ask teens to describe parental influence, anti-smoking activists insist that what moms and dads say—or don't say—can have an enormous effect on teens. In other words, parents shouldn't just breathe a sigh of relief over the new decline in smoking rates and think TV ad campaigns have more influence than they do.

The National Youth Tobacco Survey, taken every other year for the federal government, has found significant racial and ethnic differences in the ways that parents deal with smoking. Researchers say that Hispanic parents, even if they smoke themselves, are less likely to allow teens to smoke in the house. The rules appear to have the effect of discouraging teen smoking altogether, not just smoking at home, because Hispanic teens smoke at lower rates than white teens do.

Haley A.'s mother also has established a no-smoking rule at home, but the teen says there has been little discussion of the issue.

"She knows that I know about the consequences," says Haley. Although the teen doesn't particularly want to quit, she says she might be motivated to kick the habit if the penalties were severe enough. "I think if I was grounded every time I got caught smoking or if my phone got taken away, then it would definitely make it harder to keep smoking."

Keeping Teens Smoke-Free

These suggestions for parents come from Lyndon Haviland, executive vice president of the American Legacy Foundation (a public health foundation created as part of the 1998 settlement agreement by the states with the tobacco companies):

1. *Do take nicotine addiction seriously.* "When I talk to parents, I sometimes hear, 'It's only tobacco' or 'They're just experimenting,'" Haviland says. "It's critical to understand that teenagers do become addicted, and it's critical to intervene. For one thing, research shows that cigarettes can be a gateway to use of other drugs and alcohol."

2. *Don't assume teens know the dangers.* While the latest teen smoking stats are promising, there are still warning signs hidden behind the headlines. The Monitoring the Future study showed that 43 percent of eighth-graders still do not believe that there is a great risk associated with a-pack-a-day smoking.

3. *Do talk about (immediate) health consequences and the cost.* Teens tend to believe they'll never get pregnant or die in a car crash, so it may be a waste of time to talk about "someday" dying of lung cancer as a result of smoking. Instead, Haviland and other experts advise

parents to focus on short-term health and economic effects: "You get a lot of sore throats because you smoke." "If you want to run cross-country next semester, you'll have an easier time if you quit." "Your teeth are starting to get stained." Or focus on the money they're spending: "Gee, you could probably afford your own car if you weren't spending so much on cigarettes!"

4. *Don't underestimate your own influence.* "We've talked to teens who say, 'If my mom and dad really cared, they'd push me on it,'" Haviland reports.

5. *Do talk to your child's healthcare provider, athletic coaches, and guidance counselors.* The more caring adults who know your child smokes, the better, Haviland says. "You're surrounding your teen with support for cessation behavior. There is nothing wrong with saying to a soccer coach, 'My daughter will be playing on your team in the fall and I want you to know that she began smoking over the summer.'"

6. *Don't turn cigarettes into a "forbidden fruit."* No-smoking rules are fine, but only if they are premised on the dangers associated with cigarettes, not just "Those are my rules and you must obey." Make sure you tell your teen how much you admire and respect his or her decision not to smoke, or to quit.

7. *Do look for help.* The American Lung Association has a comprehensive program for teens called "NOT,"—"Not On Tobacco."

8

Easy Access to Cheap Black Market Cigarettes Encourages Teen Smoking

Dale Brazao and Robert Cribb

Dale Brazao and Robert Cribb are staff reporters for the Toronto Star.

The sale of black market cigarettes might be seen as simply a matter of circumventing the high taxes charged on tobacco products in Canada and therefore rather harmless. However, one of the main purposes for such taxes is to make cigarettes too expensive for the average teenager, and thus help discourage smoking. Black market cigarettes make smoking a very affordable habit for teens—and teens are finding them. Officials warn that black market cigarettes may be even more harmful than legal cigarettes, and have attempted to crack down on the sale of these dangerous items. Despite these efforts, black market cigarettes continue to be sold on the streets and in convenience stores.

Standing in his usual spot outside a grungy Queen St. E. bar [in Toronto], Luigi digs into his bulging coat pocket and slides a pack of illegal cigarettes into the hands of a 16-year-old.

The price is dirt cheap—$4 for 20 smokes—about half the cost of a legal pack.

Dale Brazao and Robert Cribb, "Roaring Tobacco Racket Lures Kids, Evades Taxes; Cheap 'Knock-off' Cigarettes Easier than Ever to Buy; Experts Warn of Unknown Health Risks," *The Toronto Star*, December 16, 2006, p. A01. Copyright © 2006 Toronto Star Newspapers, Ltd. Reproduced by permission of Torstar Syndication Services.

Hundreds of these transactions take place every day in Toronto's burgeoning tobacco black market—an illicit billion-dollar business that thrives by evading the taxes slapped on legal cigarettes.

Ontario's enormous—and growing—underground cigarette trade robs tens of millions from government coffers. It also undermines the "sin tax" strategy governments have long relied upon to keep teens from developing the cancer-causing habit.

The cigarettes are illegal because they are sold without government taxes; they don't display proper health warnings and are sometimes sold as singles.

The international smuggling pipeline that floods Ontario with a mind-boggling number of illegal cigarettes each year ends at corner stores, gas stations, donut shops and sidewalk merchants like Luigi.

Police and health officials have stepped up enforcement but say the problem is growing.

Of the estimated 14 billion cigarettes smoked in Ontario each year, one in four is now illegal.

The 50-something Luigi counts among his clientele men in suits, drug addicts and kids scoring a pack of cheap smokes in the middle of the day. Hour after hour, he pulls bright red packs of DK's cigarettes from his oversized blue jacket and completes the transactions.

Luigi will also sell single cigarettes for 25 cents each and cartons for $28—an array of consumer choices that has built him a bustling street-side business.

A fixture on the Queen St. E. strip east of Sherbourne St., Luigi says he's been selling illegal smokes for three months. A supplier from a native reserve drops off his shipments every couple of weeks, he said.

Black Market Cigarettes Are Big Business

Of the estimated 14 billion cigarettes smoked in Ontario each year, one in four is now illegal, according to a recently published study commissioned by Imperial Tobacco Canada—the only comprehensive research on the illicit tobacco trade, based on interviews with 2,300 adult smokers across Canada. The figure has been widely accepted by police and anti-smoking groups.

"[It is] a credible estimate of the expanding scope of illegal tobacco sales in Ontario and Quebec and should be seen as an urgent call for government action," said Cynthia Callard, executive director of Physicians for a Smoke-Free Canada.

Dave Bryans, president of the Ontario Convenience Stores Association, says his organization's research also points to a massive problem.

"We estimate 25 per cent of all cigarettes are moving illegally off of reserves in Ontario and Quebec and it's growing. No one has the will to stop the free flow of cigarettes in this province off of native reserves because they don't want to get into another native dispute. This is growing out of control."

Just go around to schools and see the discarded packs and you'll tend to see far more of the contraband brands.

RCMP [Royal Canadian Mounted Police] Supt. Joe Oliver says smugglers have close ties with organized crime. "When you're trying to cut the head of the snake, it takes time." The illegal trade "is contributing to criminal organizations and creating a very serious public safety concern ... this is not a situation where [people] are sticking it to the taxman. They're financing organized crime," he says.

There has been a 10-fold increase in contraband cigarette seizures by the RCMP in the past five years—up to 369,169 cartons last year. Provincial investigators seized another 54,800 cartons last year—five times the number of a year earlier. Experts say police seizures represent a fraction of the overall trade in illegal smokes.

RCMP generally charge alleged smugglers with unlawful possession of tobacco under the federal Excise Act. Fines on conviction can be high. First-time offenders face minimum fines of 16 cents per illegal cigarette. Repeat offenders may receive the maximum fine of 24 cents a cigarette or 90 days to 18 months in jail. The RCMP can also seize smugglers' vehicles.

At the retail level, public health inspectors can charge shopkeepers who have a business licence. They face fines of $200 to $365, seen by some as the cost of doing a brisk illegal business.

Black Market Cigarettes Are Making Their Way to Teens

Tobacco control officials say sales to minors are growing. Last year Toronto inspectors laid 264 charges against retail stores for selling to minors—more than four times the number in 2003. About one third of those relate to illegal cigarettes, said Rob Colvin, manager of healthy environments with Toronto Public Health.

"It's commonplace," he says. "Just go around to schools and see the discarded packs and you'll tend to see far more of the contraband brands."

Even stores charged for selling illegal cigarettes can't seem to quit the habit. *Toronto Star* reporters posing as consumers were easily able to buy illegal cigarettes from merchants who had been warned in the past three weeks.

The main source of illegal cigarettes in Ontario are "native" brands manufactured in factories on reserves such as Akwesasne [a Mohawk Nation Territory], which straddles the border near Cornwall. The cigarettes are labelled as DK's, Native and Chiefs among others.

But Chinese "knock-offs" of popular North American brands shipped to ports in Halifax and Vancouver are also making their way onto Toronto streets in large numbers. These counterfeits so closely resemble the real thing that smokers could be puffing away on contraband without knowing.

One reason cigarettes are so highly taxed is to keep them beyond the reach of youth.

The RCMP's Cornwall detachment, which keeps a close eye on Akwesasne's tobacco factories, seized 232,901 cartons last year representing a potential loss of nearly $10 million in tax and duty, said Sgt. Michael Harvey. In 2000, only 2,057 cartons were seized in the area.

"Five years ago there might've been one factory (on the Akwesasne reserve). Now they've got about 10 over there."

He says smugglers purchase the illegal smokes for $8 a carton on the reserve then sell them for between $22 and $23. Dubbed "runners" by police, they transport bargain-basement-priced cigarettes from reserves to retail outlets across Ontario and Quebec.

The cost to governments is staggering. Cigarettes priced as low as $3.50 in some GTA stores cost federal and provincial coffers $1.5 billion a year in lost tax revenues, according to the Imperial Tobacco Canada study.

One reason cigarettes are so highly taxed is to keep them beyond the reach of youth. At Luigi's prices, a babysitting income can finance the habit.

The *Star* sent a 16-year-old to buy from Luigi twice two weeks ago. The affable butt seller handed over the cigarettes without hesitation after collecting $4. The teen handed them to the *Star* immediately after. Toronto Public Health also uses underage shoppers to test compliance with tobacco-control bylaws.

Moments after the second sale, Luigi did brisk business selling DK's to a flock of teens.

Confronted, Luigi admitted what he's doing is against the law, but denied knowingly selling to kids. "Everybody is selling them," said Luigi. "I talked to the police about two weeks ago. They said 'Don't worry about it.' They only worry about drugs."

Toronto police say they need complaints from the public to investigate. Health officials say while they don't lay charges against street sellers such as Luigi, who don't have a business licence, they inform the RCMP.

Black Market Cigarettes Might Be More Hazardous

Health experts warn the cocktail of chemicals inside illegal cigarettes may be even more dangerous than regular smokes.

"People who buy illegal cigarettes have no idea what they're smoking," says Neil Collishaw, research director for Physicians for a Smoke-Free Canada.

Mainstream manufacturers are required to test for 44 chemicals and publicize the findings. The main ingredients— such as tar, nicotine, formaldehyde, hydrogen cyanide and carbon monoxide—must be displayed on legal packs. Not so with illegal brands such as DK's.

Illegal cigarettes are easy to find across the city. At variety stores, donut shops, dollar stores and gas bars, there are plenty of Luigis willing to risk warnings and fines.

Some carry contraband brands like Camel, Marlboro and du Maurier, apparently manufactured in Russia or China. Others sell single cigarettes, also against the law.

From the True Dollar Store on Dundas St. E., to Gerrard Convenience near Parliament St., to Super Convenience in Kensington Market, storekeepers who had already been warned by health officials for selling illegal cigarettes were still selling when the Star visited recently.

The sign outside A.J. Singh's True Dollar Store at 132 Dundas St. E. leads you to believe he has nothing for sale over $1. That obviously does not include the packs of Native and DK's he sold to a *Star* reporter on two visits.

Those transactions happened only weeks after the store was warned by city tobacco control officers about selling DK's and fake du Maurier cigarettes.

Confronted about the transactions, Singh initially said he didn't know anything about illegal cigarettes. He later called the reporter to say he had been warned by the city and while he used to sell a lot of illegal cigarettes he was now only selling them "here and there."

Across town in Kensington Market, a shopkeeper denied ever selling cigarettes to minors, minutes after she had sold a pack to Sean, 16, the non-smoking Grade 11 student the *Star* used in the undercover operation.

Leaning over a sign on her cash register forbidding sale of tobacco to anyone under 19, she was at a loss to explain why she continues to sell to minors.

At Gerrard Convenience, the owner, who identified himself only as Yang, blamed high taxes on cigarettes when asked why he sold illegal cigarettes to a reporter even after being warned by officials to stop. "The government is to blame," said Yang, who sells DK's and Chiefs. He says it's impossible to make a living selling $10 cigarettes in the neighbourhood near Regent Park. "I gotta feed my kids."

Recent busts provide some sense of the scale of illegal tobacco operations.

[In December 2006], police arrested a 19-year-old Akwesasne resident attempting to smuggle more than 700,000 cigarettes in a snowmobile trailer. Police cars boxed in the driver as he headed west on Highway 401. Police seized the cigarettes, the truck and the trailer.

In September [2006] a joint RCMP and Canada Border Service operation seized 47,580 cartons of counterfeit Players'

Light and du Maurier valued at $3.1 million. The RCMP estimates $2 million would have been evaded in federal and provincial taxes if they had hit the street.

The cigarettes had been brought from China in a container with other imported goods and were destined for a warehouse in Scarborough that was raided by the RCMP.

"From the outside of the package you wouldn't be able to tell the difference from the real cigarettes," said RCMP spokeswoman Michelle Paradis. "The packaging is that good."

Three Scarborough men were charged with unlawful possession of tobacco products.

When Ontario Provincial Police stopped two rental vans on Highway 401 near Morrisburg early last month [November 2006] they found 2,000 cartons of DK's along with 750 resealable bags of cigarettes. In all, the vans contained 550,000 illegal cigarettes destined for Toronto.

Police charged the drivers.

Three weeks ago [November 2006], RCMP officials announced they had dismantled a major cigarette and marijuana operation on the Akwesasne reserve in which the alleged "kingpin" who owned the manufacturing plant—31-year-old William Hank Cook of Cornwall—was earning $200,000 to $300,000 a week. Cook and an American man who lived on the U.S. side of Akwesasne face dozens of criminal charges.

The RCMP say the plant, MHP Manufacturing, was operating in the U.S. portion of the Akwesasne reserve. The cigarettes were smuggled across the border into Canada then trucked to various clients in Ottawa, Montreal and New Brunswick. Leaders of the Akwesasne reserve say organized crime is exploiting their community.

Meanwhile, RCMP sources say the plant is already back up and running again.

Police also charge people for being "runners." Last month, a Thunder Bay man was fined $6,500 after being found with

1,129 cartons of unmarked cigarettes. Dwayne Beauvais, a father of four, was busted after police stopped him for a traffic violation in June 2005.

Beauvis told the judge he got into cigarette smuggling because he was unemployed and had to feed his four children, three of whom suffer from serious illnesses. He was given six months to pay the reduced fine.

9

Tobacco Companies Advertise to Teenagers

Kathiann M. Kowalski

Kathiann M. Kowalski writes on a variety of topics for young people and is a member of the Society of Children's Book Writers and Illustrators.

Although tobacco companies are not allowed to advertise directly to minors, they have found effective means to sell their products to them—advertising in media for those 18 to 25. Print ads in magazines for young adults find their way into the hands of teens, and the message seen is that smoking is cool. Cigarettes are also finding their way into the hands of actors in movies aimed at young adults, which will be seen by a good number of teens. Anti-smoking campaigns have been shown to be an effective tool in the decrease in the number of teen smokers, however.

"No Boundaries. No Bull," reads the full-page cigarette ad in a recent issue of *Rolling Stone*. The tobacco company and its ad agency would say the rebellious tone of the in-your-face ad is not aimed at teens. But the magazine sits on the shelves of an Ohio public library's young adult/teen section. And the same issue carries a full-page ad for candy.

Coincidence? Probably not.

Crafty marketing? Almost certainly.

Kathiann M. Kowalski, "How Tobacco Ads Target Teens: Tobacco Companies Spend Millions of Dollars on Advertising to Hook More Smokers. Here's What You Should Know to Avoid the Lure of Tobacco," *Current Health 2*, a Weekly Reader publication. April-May, 2002, p. 6–12. Copyright © 2002 Weekly Reader Corp. Reproduced by permission.

The Hook

For decades, tobacco companies have focused marketing efforts on teens. Why? Because companies want to replace older smokers who die from tobacco-related illnesses. As a 1981 Philip Morris document said, "Today's teenager is tomorrow's potential regular customer, and the overwhelming majority of smokers first begin to smoke while in their teens."

Relatively few people start smoking or switch brands after age 18. So tobacco companies developed ad campaigns to lure teens. Themes included rugged independence, freedom, popularity, individuality, social acceptance, and carefree fun. Giveaways and promotional products became popular too. All these youth-appealing themes are still prominent in tobacco marketing.

In 1998, 46 states and the four major tobacco companies agreed to settle lawsuits for billions of dollars in tobacco-related health costs. The tobacco companies promised they would not "take any action, directly or indirectly, to target youth . . . in the advertising, promotion, or marketing of tobacco products."

Even "anti-smoking" ads sponsored by the industry can give the opposite message.

The very next year, however, the money tobacco companies spent on magazine ads shot up 33 percent to $291.1 million. Sixty percent of that went for ads in youth-oriented magazines. Those magazines have at least 15 percent or 2 million readers ages 12 to 17. In 2000, magazine ad spending dropped back near presettlement levels to $216.9 million. Spending for youth-oriented magazine ads was still 59 percent. Tobacco ads in adult magazines such as *Time* reach many teens too. The Centers for Disease Control and Prevention (CDC) estimates that tobacco advertising reaches more than 80 percent of teens.

"They're being heavily targeted by the industry," says Dr. Michael Siegel at Boston University's School of Public Health. "They need to resist and rebel against the tobacco industry's attempt to recruit them as essentially lifelong customers."

Dr. Siegel and his colleagues have documented tobacco marketing's success with teens. With cigarettes costing $3 or more per pack, price should play a big role in consumer choices. But the most popular brands among teens are the ones most heavily advertised.

Similarly, African-American teens tend to use the menthol brands advertised most in ethnically oriented magazines. "It's hard to explain the brand preferences of African-American youth on the basis of any factor other than advertising," notes Dr. Siegel.

Even "anti-smoking" ads sponsored by the industry can give the opposite message. Some ads funded by tobacco companies stress how conscientious storeowners don't sell tobacco to underage buyers. An implicit message is that smoking is a "grown-up" thing. However, three-fourths of adults don't smoke. Likewise, ads about good works by "the people at" a large tobacco company ignore the disease, pain, and suffering caused by their products.

Young people were 16 times more likely to use tobacco if their favorite actor did.

In Logan, Utah, a tobacco company gave away book covers that said, "Think. Don't Smoke." But, the word "don't" was a different color, notes 18-year-old Marin Poole, "So THINK SMOKE stood out." One design featured an angry snowboarder. "The snowboard looked like a lit match, and the clouds looked more like smoke than clouds," Marin says. Her campaign to get the book covers out of Logan High School, plus other anti-smoking efforts, earned her the Campaign for Tobacco-Free Kids' 2001 Youth Advocate of the Year award for the western region.

Cynthia Loesch won the award for the eastern region. In 1998, her group persuaded a major Boston newspaper to stop accepting tobacco ads. Cynthia continues to educate people—both adults and youth—about tobacco. "It's a fact that cigarettes do absolutely nothing for you, and all they lead to is illnesses and eventually death," says Cynthia.

Star Struck

Stars smoking in films or off-screen include Leonardo Di Caprio, Neve Campbell, Sylvester Stallone, Gillian Anderson, Ashley Judd, Sean Penn, John Travolta, and more. In a recent Dartmouth University study, young people were 16 times more likely to use tobacco if their favorite actor did. In another Dartmouth study, middle school students allowed to watch R-rated films (more inclined to show smoking and drinking) were five times more likely to try cigarettes and alcohol than those whose parents wouldn't let them watch R-rated films.

Even G, PG, and PG-13 movies often show tobacco use. In *The Muppet Movie*, for example, three cigar-smoking humans interacted with the Muppets.

"When movie stars are smoking in their movies or in front of young people, they're almost just as responsible as the tobacco industry is for addicting young people," maintains 17-year-old Shannon Brewer, the 2001 National Youth Advocate of the Year for the Campaign for Tobacco-Free Kids. "Whether or not they use it all the time, it's an influence on kids because it's saying that's what it takes in order to be that star."

Of course, not all actors smoke—and some take a stand against tobacco and other drugs. Actor Jeremy London, model Christy Turlington, and various other celebrities, for example, work with the CDC, American Lung Association, or Campaign for Tobacco-Free Kids to present positive role models.

Yet too many moviemakers use cigarettes and cigars as quick cliche props. "If they're creative producers and directors, they should be able to portray attractive characters through other means," challenges Dr. Siegel.

Why Should You Worry?

Very few legal products are deadly when used as directed. Tobacco, however, is America's No. 1 killer. According to the CDC, 430,000 Americans die each year from tobacco-related causes. Inhaled smoke and chewed tobacco directly affect the user. Secondhand smoke affects people who live, work, or socialize with smokers.

Nicotine is tobacco's addictive "hook." At least 63 of the other 4,000 chemicals in tobacco cause cancer, according to the American Lung Association. The list of toxic ingredients also includes tar, carbon monoxide, arsenic, hydrogen cyanide, acetylene, benzene, and formaldehyde.

Lung cancer and cancers of the stomach, pancreas, mouth, throat, and esophagus are all linked to tobacco. Tobacco also kills by causing heart attacks, strokes, and other circulatory diseases.

Besides direct deaths, tobacco makes people more susceptible to bronchitis, pneumonia, asthma, and other illnesses. Tobacco reduces lung capacity and impairs an athlete's performance. Smoking during pregnancy increases risks of miscarriage, premature birth, and sudden infant death syndrome (SIDS).

Tobacco messes with your mind too. Some teen smokers say smoking relaxes them. But researcher Andy Parrott at the University of East London found that teen smokers' stress levels increased as regular smoking patterns developed. Any perceived relaxation was just temporary relief of nicotine with-drawal between cigarettes. In short, cigarette smoking caused stress.

In another study reported by the American Academy of Pediatrics, teen smokers were nearly four times as likely as nonsmokers to develop serious symptoms of depression. Depression is a mental illness that hampers day-to-day functioning. Severe cases can even lead to suicide.

Beyond this, tobacco stains teeth and nails. It dulls skin and hair. Smoke reeks and lingers on hair and clothing. Instead of making people attractive, smoking does just the opposite.

Nasty Nicotine

About 60 percent of current teen smokers have tried to quit within the past year, reports the CDC. Most started out thinking they could quit at any time. But nicotine addiction seizes control before teens realize they're hooked—sometimes within days or weeks after the first cigarette.

Pure nicotine is deadly. Tobacco, however, delivers just enough nicotine (1 to 2 mg in the average cigarette) to hook users. You might say that cigarettes are engineered as highly effective drug delivery devices.

Teens who regularly receive anti-smoking messages are twice as likely not to smoke as teens who don't get that exposure.

The National Institute on Drug Abuse reports that nicotine increases dopamine levels in the brain's "reward circuits" within 10 seconds of inhaling. The neurotransmitter dopamine increases feelings of pleasure. Nicotine also decreases the brain's levels of monoamine oxidase (MAO), an enzyme that breaks down excess dopamine.

Nicotine's peak effects dissipate within minutes. Users then need more nicotine to sustain the feeling. So, they smoke more. Depending on a person's arousal state, nicotine can be both a stimulant and a sedative.

When addicted users don't get nicotine, they experience withdrawal. Symptoms include cravings, anxiety, nervousness, and irritability. Thanks to nicotine, the tobacco industry often hooks customers for life.

Knowledge Is Power

Media messages that show tobacco favorably entice teens to smoke. But anti-smoking advertising can counter those influences. Dr. Siegel and his colleagues found that teens who regularly receive anti-smoking messages are twice as likely not to smoke as teens who don't get that exposure.

Instead of thinking that "everybody" smokes, teens were more likely to believe that only about one-fourth of American adults and teens smoke—which is true. In other words, getting the facts about smoking helps teens tell the difference between tobacco companies' media myths and reality, notes Dr. Siegel.

In fact, researchers at the University of Michigan found that from 1996 to 2001 the percentage of eighth graders who were smoking dropped to 12 percent from 21 percent; tenth graders who were smoking fell to 21 percent, down from 30 percent. Among 12th graders, the number of smokers dropped to 30 percent in 2001, down from a 37 percent peak in 1997. This drop in teen smoking is attributed to anti-smoking campaigns.

Anti-smoking ordinances and restaurant bans help too. Such rules reduce bystanders' exposure to secondhand smoke. Plus, they keep people from being constantly assaulted by tobacco's pervasive odor. "In towns that don't allow smoking in restaurants," notes Dr. Siegel, "kids are more likely to perceive that fewer people in their community smoke. They're not constantly smelling it and being exposed to it."

10

Antismoking Campaigns Can Be Effective with Teenagers

Beth Herskovits

Beth Herskovits writes for PR Week.

Effectively reaching young people with antismoking messages re-quires a sophisticated approach—something more than simply telling them that they should not smoke because "it is bad for you." The American Legacy Foundation's "Truth" campaign employs savvy marketing strategies to reach youth: Web sites, online video games, "Truth"-branded items, as well as a focus on at-risk teenagers.

More than an anti-smoking campaign, the American Legacy Foundation's "Truth" effort has become a brand in its own right.

Past Truth ads have peeled away the layers of tobacco companies' marketing tactics. One spot, for instance, questioned the altruism of a company that spent 21 million dollars publicizing a 125,000 dollar charitable donation. Another featured orange arrows branding unsuspecting people as "passive-aggressive" or "emotionally insecure," terms from the tobacco industry's own files.

But to reach teen audiences, the foundation must constantly make sure that it is keeping up with—and indeed, even getting one step ahead of—youth marketing trends and finding new ways to present the same old message: Smoking is bad for you.

Joe Martyak, EVP of marketing, communications, and public policy, stresses how Legacy strives to keep up with "the chameleon aspect" of young people. To that end, the foundation last month launched the next evolution of Truth: the "Truth documentary."

Reaching Teens Where They Live

The initiative, aimed at 12- to 17-year-olds, includes materials, such as TV spots and a new Web site, www.whadufxup.com, that show Gen Y types reacting to the language and marketing tactics tobacco companies use to attract and keep teens as smokers.

"When we go out with information, it's well-founded, it's well-sourced. It's our modus operandi," Martyak says. He adds that research, legal, and programming teams work closely together. "It's all integrated communications. It's really synergistic among those three."

Legacy is also using the same technology as teens. In February, for instance, it incorporated elements of the Truth campaign into video games. It is also looking at how it can use new media and text messages.

The challenge is overcoming the perception that smoking is sexy and cool.

An annual summer Truth tour—which Legacy is bringing this year [2006] to about 58 cities—is a key component of its outreach. In addition to working with local media, the PR team also plans to pitch teen magazines on the gear that will be given out during the events. The idea is to get teens to see Truth as a hot brand before the tour hits town. The tour reached over 800,000 teens last year [2005].

Martyak notes that Truth is recognized by 80% of teens and is one of the 10 most memorable teen brands. It also has an underground quality. "A lot of parents do not even know what Truth is," he explains.

But Legacy doesn't try to be all things to all teens. "We focus most narrowly on teens who are most likely to smoke," he says.

Legacy works with agencies that target what it calls "priority populations," which focus on audiences of different ethnicities or sexual orientations, for example.

"The Truth effort has been the envy of the entire public health community," says Greg Donaldson, national communications VP at the American Cancer Society (ACS). "[It's] very relevant, very contemporary."

"They are a very sophisticated, well-oiled machine," says Laurie Fenton, president of the Lung Cancer Alliance. "The challenge is overcoming the perception that smoking is sexy and cool. [Truth] is just a very powerful, provocative campaign."

While Truth is a youth brand, Legacy has also built cessation programs. "Though we don't talk to parents specifically, we do talk to adults," says Patricia McLaughlin, senior director of communications.

Although Legacy had always led with the Truth brand in the past, it is now working to promote the parent brand to the media and policymakers.

How Legacy Came to Be

The organization has a unique history. It was founded in 1999 as a result of the Master Settlement Agreement between the tobacco industry and 46 state attorneys general. A provision called for tobacco companies to fund youth anti-smoking programs.

The group received its last payment in 2003 and has been challenged to raise its own funds. It is also engaged in a four-year legal battle with Lorillard Tobacco Co., which has argued that Legacy's ads attack the company and its employees.

Final appeals are currently being heard in front of the Delaware Supreme Court.

"If Lorillard were to win, that would basically shut our doors," says Julia Cartwright. SVP of communications. "Every time we can get [reporters] to get some of this information out—well-placed and accurate—that's a milestone, as far as I'm concerned."

Legacy doesn't lobby, but policy changes on the Hill certainly shape its message. "We collaborate on an ongoing basis," says ACS's Donaldson. "We understand that the fight against tobacco is a multifaceted effort."

Legacy worked recently with state attorneys general to announce that US cigarette sales have decreased—which resulted in stories above the fold in the *Washington Post* and the *New York Times*.

"PR is critical for the public understanding of what we do," Martyak says.

11

School Cessation Programs May Reduce Teen Smoking

Lini S. Kadaba

Lini S. Kadaba is a staff writer for the Philadelphia Inquirer.

Until recently, high schools have dealt with teen smoking by means of antismoking rules and punishment for infractions of those rules. This approach, however, has not seen a decrease in the number of teen smokers. Some high schools are now taking a different approach—helping students who already smoke to kick the habit. Smoking cessation programs are being offered in school as a means to curtail student smoking.

For years, high schooler David Collins has heard about the evils of smoking.

Smoking kills 440,000 Americans each year. Cigarettes contain at least 43 cancer-causing chemicals. Nicotine is addictive.

It didn't matter. Like many teens, the junior at Devon Preparatory School smoked anyway, taking his first drag at age 10. "It was forbidden," he said. "It was cool." His habit took a pack-a-week hold through much of high school—until now.

Collins, 17, wants to quit, and he's turning to his school for help. There, he attends a new smoking cessation program during the academic day, part of a growing, national effort to help youths, some as young as middle schoolers, stop smoking.

Prevention has long been the focus of antismoking efforts in the nation's schools. Now, some are acknowledging that they must also help students who already smoke learn how to quit.

I kind of needed to stop. And it's disgusting. I was running out of money all the time.

Helping Teens Kick the Habit

To accomplish this, schools are turning to a host of curriculum-based smoking-cessation programs designed with teens in mind. The success rate is hard to measure, and some efforts are proving controversial because they are partially sponsored by tobacco companies. But counselors and students involved in the programs give them high marks.

"I play a lot of sports," said Collins of Exton, who attends Ending Nicotine Dependence (END). "I kind of needed to stop. And it's disgusting. I was running out of money all the time."

Although tobacco use among youths has declined since 1996, many still light up, according to the 2000 National Youth Tobacco Survey. It found that 11 percent of middle schoolers and 28 percent of high schoolers smoke.

The most helpful thing they teach is how to quit.

With those statistics in mind, schools are turning to END, N-O-T (Not On Tobacco), and other cessation curriculums.

"Most teens who have been smoking for any number of years are tired of burn holes in jeans and money going out," said Linda Stezelberger, a regional program director for the American Lung Association of Pennsylvania, which developed the N-O-T program. "Most older teens want to quit."

But recruitment can be tough, facilitators say, because teens often see smoking as cool and not addictive—and cessation programs as uncool. To get teens to join, some agencies are backing away from requiring parental permission, and some schools describe the programs as tobacco education.

Even those teens who sign on don't always have an easy ride.

"It's not a quick fix," allowed Susan Pizzi, community health education coordinator at Chester County Hospital, which has taken the 10-week N-O-T class to West Chester schools. "It may take a few times to quit."

Amie D'Annunzio, 17, a Downingtown High School junior, said the program had taught her to break certain routines, such as smoking after school.

"I haven't quit, but I've cut back a lot," she said. "They tell you the bad effects, but a lot of that we've heard for years. The most helpful thing they teach is how to quit."

The weekly programs offered over two to three months do not insist students stop, but try to move them closer to that goal.

The jury, however, is out on the success rate.

"There's very little evidence that any of them work to reduce smoking," said Cheryl Healton, head of the American Legacy Foundation, which was established under the $206 billion tobacco settlement reached in 1998 by 46 states, including Pennsylvania and New Jersey.

Tobacco settlement money is largely driving the spread of youth cessation programs.

Still, Healton emphasized that studies were under way and that the programs were worthwhile because adolescents learn skills that increase their chances of eventually quitting. The Legacy Foundation plans to launch Circle of Friends, its own youth cessation program.

Offering Help Rather Than Punishing Smokers

Schools are welcoming the programs, in some cases as an alternative to punitive measures.

Upper Darby High School offers smoking cessation in place of hefty fines. At St. Joseph's Preparatory School in Philadelphia, students caught smoking must attend the END program instead of after-school detention, counselor Cheryl Thomas said.

"They're students," she said, "and we need to let them know what choices they have."

Tobacco settlement money is largely driving the spread of youth cessation programs, health officials said. The five-county region received $8.9 million in the 2001–02 fiscal year for prevention and cessation for all ages; a similar amount is allotted for this fiscal year. Comparable numbers were not available for South Jersey, but statewide, $30 million will go to various tobacco initiatives, including smoking cessation.

The Caron Foundation, a 45-year-old drug-treatment center based in Wernersville, Berks County, teaches the END curriculum in several states and at schools in the region through a grant from Philip Morris USA. The curriculum was developed by the Utah Department of Health.

The American Lung Association and the Legacy Foundation oppose tobacco company support of such programs. "It is not in the tobacco companies' interest to have teens quit," Stezelberger said. "It's a way of dooming any success of cessation."

But, said Mylene Krzanowski, Caron's director of student assistance programs, "I know at the end of the day that that money is being used in a pertinent and meaningful manner. We're able to help a lot of kids."

A Philip Morris spokeswoman said the Caron grant was part of its commitment to prevent youths from smoking.

Cessation Programs in Action

Devon Prep's school nurse, Denise Gavin, welcomed the END program to the school, noting the tobacco company's name did not appear on literature she reviewed.

At a recent session in the Devon Prep cafeteria, six students discussed sources of stress that trigger smoking: SATs, after-school activities and parents.

Amy Mack, a social worker with Caron who easily talked with the teens, suggested more exercise, healthier diets, fewer after-school activities.

Senior Andrew Egan, 18, of Malvern, a pack-a-day smoker, wants to quit because "I couldn't play sports anymore. I didn't have the energy."

Drew Turner, 17, a junior from West Chester, said he never had a reason to quit—until a relative died from emphysema. "I figured I'm not going to smoke and die like my grandfather."

12

Changing State Laws May Reduce Teen Smoking

Patrik Jonsson

Patrik Jonsson is a staff writer for the Christian Science Monitor.

South Carolina, a major tobacco-producing state, recently out-lawed possession of tobacco by teenagers (nearly every other state in the country has had such laws on the books for many years). Seen as a major victory over tobacco lobbyists, the health care community anticipates that this legislation will lead the way to a reduction in the number of teen smokers in the state.

In [August 2006] the state [South Carolina] finally outlawed underage smoking. Critics say that's not enough.

With the lowest cigarette tax in the nation and a dead-last ranking in smoking prevention, South Carolina remains one of the last true smokers' outposts.

But from the Pee Dee River to Parris Island, the Palmetto State's "smoke-and-let-smoke" ethic is changing—at least when it comes to teenage partakers. By becoming one of the last states to outlaw teenage possession of tobacco on Aug. 21, the legislature and Gov. Mark Sanford (Republican) took the state's first tentative steps toward state-sponsored smoking prevention.

The gambit itself won't likely change many minds. In fact, critics expect police won't find much time to impose a $25 fine, up to five days of community service, and possibly a lecture from the judge's bench on an underage smoker. Yet experts say the law does have meaning, not only for parents trying to bolster their own "don't smoke" sermons, but for an antismoking movement that, until now, has failed to gain purchase in a state that perhaps takes tobacco more seriously than any other.

When it comes to South Carolina teens, one in four of them have smoked in the last 30 days compared to a national average of just over one in five.

"There's a wide variety in states about the level of legislative activism [on tobacco]," says Dick Vallandingham, director of prevention services for the Beaufort County Alcohol and Drug Abuse Department. "But even if you're at the tail end like South Carolina and you've got your feet dragging the back end of the wagon, you're still in the wagon."

Poor people smoke more than rich people, which is one reason why South Carolina, one of the nation's poorest states, has a higher-than-average smoking rate. Kentucky has the highest overall smoking rate—just under 30 percent in 2004, according to the state's health department.

When it comes to South Carolina teens, one in four of them have smoked in the last 30 days compared to a national average of just over one in five, according to the Campaign for Tobacco-Free Kids.

Facing Off with a Tobacco Culture

But there's more to the story. As August winds down, the fertile 14-county Pee Dee River region is in the midst of hauling another season's worth of "leaf"—a pungent, social tradition dating back more than 300 years. So protective of tobacco is the legislature that it has bucked even the tobacco industry by refusing to put tax stamps on its cigarette packs. Such stamps allow authorities to track the movement of large purchases of cigarettes, especially from a cheap-tobacco state like South Carolina.

A victory by the health lobby in South Carolina means a strike at the very heart of what remains of America's tobacco culture.

What's more, the state won't let communities enact their own no-smoking laws, despite efforts by lawmakers in the two largest cities—Columbia and Charleston—to do just that.

That in part explains why, instead of raising the cigarette tax above the current 7 cents and airing gritty public service announcements about the realities of smoking—two of the tactics credited with the drastic national dip in teen smoking over the last 10 years—South Carolina is dusting off an idea that has had little real impact on teen smoking when tried in other states, critics say.

"The [teen smoking law] is actually a sign that South Carolina has an old school tobacco control policy that other states were doing 10, 15 years ago," says Amy Barkley, a state advocacy director for the Campaign for Tobacco-Free Kids. "What it does is give [tobacco supporters] an excuse not to do things that are more effective."

The teen-smoking crackdown in South Carolina comes at a peculiar time for the smoking debate in America. Teen smoking rates dropped rapidly after states began focusing on the issue around 1996. But those rates have now flattened out as states like Florida and Massachusetts drastically cut their prevention efforts. A victory by the health lobby in South Carolina means a strike at the very heart of what remains of America's tobacco culture.

"In a state as impoverished as South Carolina, with escalating costs of health care, the tobacco issue is as volatile an issue now as it was 15 years ago," says Fred Carter, a political science professor and president of Francis Marion University in Florence, S.C. "While the health lobby is inclined to take some steps, it doesn't have enough clout to take on the tobacco industry and do something that would have a lasting and irrevocable impact on anti-smoking efforts, which is raising the cigarette tax."

Twenty-something Amanda Taylor, who started smoking young, says South Carolina remains a smoker's mecca. Yet outlawing possession for high school students may be an effective deterrent—and certainly won't hurt, Ms. Taylor says. "It's probably a good message to send," she says.

In Marion County, in the heart of the Pee Dee region, Jerry Battle, a Democratic state legislator who runs a tobacco warehouse, acknowledges South Carolina's peculiar leanings, as well as its social and cultural protection of the leaf.

Yet even Mr. Battle sees the smoke clearing somewhat over the Palmetto State. To be sure, the fight over whether to promote or denounce tobacco—either overtly or covertly—will go on because it's a point of pride and principle on Tobacco Road, he says.

But "the industry is concerned and I really honestly think that you're going to see stronger efforts coming out of South Carolina to temper teenage smoking," says Battle.

"At the same time, I think adults should have the freedom to smoke and not become second-class citizens just because this is something we do, he says."

13

Reducing Teen Smoking Will Require New and Creative Strategies

Robert Worth

Robert Worth was an editor of the Washington Monthly *from 1998 to 1999. He is now a staff writer for the* New York Times.

Laws alone are not enough to curtail teen smoking. The problem with teenage smoking is not that the tobacco industry tries to peddle their cigarettes to that age group, but rather that smoking is seen as being "cool." Prohibition runs counter to the way teenagers think and can have the unwanted effect of actually encouraging young people to smoke. To see real declines in the number of young people using tobacco, society will need to approach the subject in a way that appeals to the way teens see the world and to their priorities. The author argues that the best way to stop teenage smoking is to make smoking look ridiculous, which can be challenging when much of popular culture depicts smoking as "cool."

L aughter is our best weapon in the war on teen smoking.

On the surface, November's [1999] $206 billion settlement agreement between the tobacco companies and 46 states looks like a serious blow for Big Tobacco. In addition to the money, it contains some important concessions: a ban on outdoor advertising, limits on sports sponsorships and merchandising, no more "product placement" in movies, and they have to close The Tobacco Institute and other junk-science instruments. And Joe Camel—along with all other cartoon characters—is gone for good.

Teenagers will find ways to smoke, no matter how many public service announcements or laws are written to stop them.

Yet how much did all this hurt the tobacco industry's ability to sell cigarettes? On November 20, [1999] the day the attorneys general announced the settlement, the stock of the leading tobacco companies soared. After all, the Big Four tobacco makers will pay only 1 percent of the damages (at most) directly; the rest will be passed on to smokers through higher prices. Since many states are already figuring the settlement money into their budgets, this puts them in the odd position of depending on the continued health of the tobacco industry for their roads, schools, and hospitals.

Punishing the industry, in other words, doesn't necessarily address the root of the problem—reducing demand for cigarettes. And that won't go down until we all face the fact that smoking is once again cool. When I went to high school, in the 1980s, scarcely any of my classmates smoked. My two teenage cousins claim that at least half of their friends smoke, despite a heavy barrage of anti-smoking publicity. They're not unusual: According to the Centers for Disease Control and Prevention (CDC), teen smoking rose 73 percent from 1988 to 1996.

Anti-smoking activists often behave as though the tobacco companies were entirely to blame for this fact—as though charisma were a substance like nicotine that could be injected and removed from a product at will. Sadly, that's not true. As long as movie stars like John Travolta and Uma Thurman flirt gorgeously through a haze of cigarette smoke, as long as it drifts through all the right nightclubs and bars and hang-outs—not to mention the magazines and posters and bill-boards—teenagers will find ways to smoke, no matter how many public service announcements or laws are written to stop them. Most of these kids know that smoking fills their lungs with toxins like arsenic, cyanide, and formaldehyde. They'll even recite the statistics to you: Smoking kills over 1,000 people a day in this country alone, and is far deadlier, in terms of mortality rates, than any hard drug. And then they'll blow their smoke into your face. "Kids can't imagine them-selves old," says Stanton Glantz, an anti-smoking activist and professor at the University of California at San Francisco. "Health effects mean almost nothing to them."

Fight Fire with Fire

The only way to get any leverage with teenagers is to return fire with fire, taking on the various influences that make smok-ing seem attractive. We need, in other words, to find new ways to make smoking look ridiculous.

As it happens, we have some clues about how to do that. Flash back to the 1960s, when cigarette ads were as common on television as they are now on billboards or bus-stops. If you ask any man in his 40s or older about the tobacco ads of that day, he'll almost certainly remember one series in par-ticular: the Marlboro Man ads. Set to the music from the great Western *The Magnificent Seven*, they brought the cel-ebrated smoking cowboy to life as he roped calves in a gold and red-hued western sunset. They conjured up the untram-meled masculinity of the cowboy myth so masterfully that few who ever saw them have forgotten them. And their message was unmistakable: Real men smoke.

Then, in 1968, another ad appeared on television. This one began with a cowboy standing in a darkened saloon, watched by a low-life villain with a gun (and a cigarette in his mouth). Another gunslinger enters, a cigarette hanging from his lips. "We figured you'd be here," he tells the hero. The bad men are on the verge of gunning the hero down, when one of them begins to wheeze. Soon both of them are doubling over in coughing fits, and the hero strolls past them, unharmed, out of the saloon. The words "American Cancer Society" appear on the screen, and the announcer intones "Cigarettes—they're killers."

The industry figured that once those pesky counter-ads were gone the decline in smoking would stop. They were right.

This ad may seem laughably unsophisticated to the current generation of media-soaked teenagers, but in its day it managed to make the Marlboro Man ads look utterly ridiculous. And along with a group of similarly inspired antismoking ads that ran at the same time, it appears to have had a measurable effect. Starting in 1967, when the anti-smoking ads first aired on television, and ending in 1970, when they went off, per capita cigarette consumption dropped four years in a row—something that had not happened since the turn of the century. Naturally, there were other reasons for this decline, but researchers tend to agree that the ads were a powerful factor. They also permeated the culture in ways that can't be quantified, making people less likely to associate cigarettes with glamour. In Hollywood movies, where smoking had been de rigeur for decades, cigarettes disappeared like the hats from mens' heads. Only 29 percent of movie characters smoked in the 1970s, according to Stanton Glantz—less than half as many as before or since.

That's why the best thing in last November's settlement may be its creation of a national foundation, funded at $25 million a year, designed to "Develop, disseminate, and test the effectiveness of counter advertising campaigns." If we can use that money to create an ad campaign as powerful as the one that aired three decades ago, we just might kill the Marlboro myth for good.

Equal Time

The first great antismoking ad campaign began on Thanksgiving Day 1966, when a young lawyer named John Banzhaf III was watching a football game. A cigarette ad came on—probably for Marlboros. It showed "handsome, rugged men confidently smoking cigarettes in an outdoor western setting. It implied that any man who wanted to be truly masculine should smoke cigarettes." It made Banzhaf mad, and he decided to "do whatever I could to wipe out those evil commercials." He chose as his weapon the Federal Communications Commission's now-defunct Fairness Doctrine, which held that when covering controversial topics broadcasters had to give time to opposing views. It had never been applied to commercials before, but the FCC ruled in Banzhaf's favor. By 1967 broadcasters were airing one anti-smoking ad for every four cigarette ads, on prime time television.

Most of the ads were produced by the American Cancer Society and the American Lung Association, and they were so good that the tobacco industry began to panic. "The opinion of many top-level tobacco people," one former tobacco executive told a reporter in 1969, "is that as things stand they'd just as soon have cigarette commercials banned if by that they could in effect get the anti-smoking commercials banned, too." When it became clear that smoking rates were indeed dropping, the tobacco chiefs asked Congress to ban them from television, much against the will of the broadcasters, who stood to lose hundreds of millions of dollars a year. (The tobacco companies didn't want to withdraw voluntarily, because that might confer a market advantage on those who stayed.) The industry figured that once those pesky counter-ads were gone the decline in smoking would stop. They were right.

They were clever too, because cigarettes didn't really disappear from television. With all the money they saved on ads (close to $800 million a year in current dollars), the tobacco companies managed to make sure that major sports events would occur against the backdrop of a massive cigarette ad. They sponsored tennis tournaments and drag races; they poured ads into newspapers and magazines; they papered highways and inner cities with untold acres of billboards. They crafted new brands to specific demographics—Eve, Misty, and Capri for women, following the 1968 launch of Virginia Slims; Uptown and Kool for blacks; American Spirit for native Americans.

By the 1980s, the tobacco industry was reclaiming Hollywood with a full-court effort to "place" their products in movies. One of the documents uncovered in Minnesota's suit against the industry last year made this particularly graphic, stating that "product was supplied" by Phillip Morris for more than 190 movies between 1978 and 1988. The company calls them "donations," and it's true that no records of payment were ever found. But if that's true, why did the same company shell out $350,000 to place Lark cigarettes in the James Bond film *License to Kill* in 1988?

The anti-smoking movement itself probably deserves some of the blame for recent increases in teen smoking.

Movie industry spokesmen claim that product placement hasn't happened since 1990, and last November's settlement explicitly forbids it. And it should be said that Hollywood directors are far more likely to be slaves to fashion than to the tobacco industry. But whatever the reason, by the mid-1990s, Hollywood movies were once again filled with smoke. According to the American Lung Association, in 133 top movies produced in 1994 and 1995, 82 percent of the lead or supporting characters smoke.

When challenged about their use of cigarettes in films, directors tend to offer the excuse that smoking is sometimes necessary to build character. If that's true, why wasn't it the case in the 1970s? After all, that decade produced some of the greatest movies of recent times. In some popular movies of the past few years, the smoking seems laughably gratuitous. Couldn't James Cameron have found a more interesting way of manifesting Leonardo DiCaprio's rebelliousness in *Titanic* than by having him smoke like a chimney? In *My Best Friend's Wedding* Julia Roberts chain-smokes despite the fact that she's playing a food critic. Many of these directors aren't really worried about building character; they're just plain lazy.

Actors and directors also tend to downplay their influence over kids. "I don't apologize for smoking onscreen," Winona Ryder told *USA Today* last year. "It should be our choice, and I don't think we influence people to smoke." Maybe so. But consider: The Ray Ban company saw 55 percent gains after Tom Cruise donned a pair of their sunglasses in *Risky Business* Sales of Reese's Pieces candy jumped 65 percent after they appeared in Stephen Spielberg's blockbuster *E.T.* Why should cigarettes be any different?

Up in Smoke

In fairness to Hollywood, the anti-smoking movement itself probably deserves some of the blame for recent increases in teen smoking. Like so many social crusaders before them, they've occasionally lapsed into self-righteousness—thereby inviting teens to take up cigarettes as the torch of fashionable rebellion. They have supported laws that allow police to arrest and fine teenagers caught with cigarettes—a foolish strategy that blames the young smoker instead of the marketers. They have encouraged businesses to discriminate against smokers.

They have lobbied to have cigarettes regulated like hard drugs, or even banned outright—thereby demonstrating that they've learned nothing from the War on Drugs, or, for that matter, from the great failed experiment in temperance that began in 1919. "They have become prohibitionists," says Dr. Alan Blum, a Baylor physician who is one of the greatest and most clear-eyed anti-smoking activists. In the process, they've only hurt themselves—because once you start acting like Miss Watson you cast smokers in the role of Huckleberry Finn.

How, then, to persuade teenagers not to pick up the habit? ... The best approach seems to be the one that worked back in the late '60s: satire.

The tobacco companies, never slow to learn a PR lesson, have worked hard in recent years to dress their product as forbidden fruit. They've supported laws that allow police to arrest and fine teenagers caught with cigarettes, and promised not to oppose them as part of last November's settlement. And they've launched massive campaigns that are designed, supposedly, to combat teen smoking. The new $100 million Phillip Morris campaign, which had its television launch in December, is titled "Think, Don't Smoke," and it focuses on persuading teens to resist peer pressure.

Think? Resist peer pressure? This is a little like marketing chastity belts; you create an incentive where there may not have been one. The truth is that most teenagers don't feel much peer pressure to smoke, because the majority of teens don't do it. But with the tobacco companies telling them they've got to exercise massive self-restraint in order to not smoke, well, hey—maybe it's worth trying after all.

The R.J. Reynolds anti-smoking campaign is equally disingenuous. It's true, as one RJR spokesman told me, that they've mailed out half a million "We Card" kits to retailers. But the premise of the campaign—that parents should simply tell their children not to smoke—is absurd. "We have a unit on how to talk to your kids about smoking even if you do smoke," the spokesman told me.

Ultimately, this message is just a subtler form of marketing. "When I was a kid it was 'Lucky Strike separates the men from the boys,'" the great anti-smoking ad writer Tony Schwartz told me. "Now [the tobacco companies] tell people 'Kids shouldn't smoke, that's for adults.' Isn't the message the same?" Ironically, the very first television anti-smoking commercial, which Schwartz created in 1963, hit this theme. The ad featured a pair of children dressing up in their parents' clothes—long white dress for the girl, suit and top hat for the boy, and posing in front of a mirror. "Children love to imitate their parents," the announcer says. "Children learn by imitating their parents. Do you smoke cigarettes?"

This ad, which ran frequently during the late '60s, is often cited as one of the great PR successes of that era. Unfortunately, it doesn't answer the question of how to reach kids themselves.

Ads feature a cancer-victim singing "Happy Birthday" to the tobacco industry through his throat-hole.

Mocking Word

How, then, to persuade teenagers not to pick up the habit? There's no single formula, says Jeff McKenna, director of the Centers for Disease Control and Preventions Office of Smoking and Health, which tracks anti-smoking efforts and their effectiveness. But the best approach seems to be the one that worked back in the late '60s: satire. California, which funds anti-smoking commercials with the proceeds of a 25-cent cigarette surtax passed in 1988, has led the way in this area. One of their recent ads features a group of dapper young men in tuxes who light their cigarettes as a gorgeous young woman walks in. As the announcer tells us about the link between smoking and impotence, their cigarettes suddenly go limp—and the woman looks mockingly at them and walks away. "Cigarettes," the announcer says. "Still think they're sexy?"

Direct satires of the tobacco industry have also been touted as a way to persuade kids that smoking isn't as rebellious as they may think. "What we've found is that when kids understand they're being manipulated by the industry, it takes the desirability of the rebellion away," says Colleen Stevens, who directs the California Health Department's antismoking media campaign. The first and most celebrated ad in the California television campaign hit this theme hard. It shows a smoky boardroom full of tobacco executives, one of whom announces: "Gentlemen, gentlemen, the tobacco industry has a very serious multi-billion dollar problem . . . Every day 2,000 Americans stop smoking and another 1,100 also quit. Actually, technically, they die. That means this business needs 3,000 fresh volunteers every day. So forget about all that heart disease, cancer, emphysema, and stroke stuff. We're not in this business for our health." Another ad simply showed footage of tobacco industry executives testifying before Congress that they believed tobacco was not addictive. The words "under oath" flash on the screen during the testimony, and as the ad closes the announcer intones: "Now the tobacco industry is trying to tell us that second hand smoke isn't dangerous."

More recently, other states have followed California's lead. Massachusetts, which passed its own cigarette surtax in 1992, ran an ad featuring Victor D. Noble, a scientist who did important work on the health risks of smoking, telling the camera how the tobacco industry shut him down. Another shows Victor Crawford, a former tobacco lobbyist, confessing "I lied." Other ads feature a cancer-victim singing "Happy Birthday" to the tobacco industry through his throat-hole; a child smoking, accompanied by the legend "They knew. They always knew"; and a quote from an RJR draft memo suggesting that warning labels on cigarette packs could actually be an enticement to kids. Last year Florida used the money from its own separate settlement with the industry to establish a campaign directed by teenagers. Designated the "Truth" campaign, it is explicitly targeted at the tobacco industry's alleged manipulation of kids.

It's too early to tell how effective these efforts will be, but the early signs from California—the longest-running campaign—are good. Since it began, teen smoking in California has remained stable, even as it shot up in the rest of the country. The overall effect has been even more striking: Cigarette consumption has declined by 38 percent, or more than twice as much as the 16 percent decline in the rest of the country. Although the Massachusetts campaign is younger, it appears to have been effective too; teen smoking rates have risen far less than in the rest of the country.

If attacking the industry proves consistently to be the best way to cut teen smoking rates, then there's no reason not to do it.

Both states are quick to point out that media campaigns aren't everything; they've also worked hard to restrict smoking in public places, and to create education and community programs. Still, the power of the ads can be measured by what happened when they went off the air in California. Soon after the ad featuring the Congressional tobacco testimony first appeared, R.J. Reynolds threatened to sue both the state department of health services and the stations that aired it. The health department stood firm, and Reynolds backed down. But Gov. Pete Wilson (who's been described in internal Phillip Morris documents as "tobacco-friendly") pressured the department to stop running its anti-industry satires. He also insisted that the health department not use the words "lies" or "tobacco industry" in any of its ads, and he began to drain off the money allocated for the antismoking campaign for other purposes. Soon afterward, cigarette consumption began to rise, and youth smoking rates climbed nearly 20 percent.

Putting It Out

These campaigns represent a promising start. But as the California example suggests, they're vulnerable to political meddling. At the national level too, the tobacco industry, with typical agility, has found a way to undermine them. Buried deep in last November's settlement agreement is a clause stating that the money spent on anti-smoking ads through a national foundation created by the settlement for that purpose shall be used "only for public education and advertising regarding the addictiveness, health effects, and social costs related to the use of tobacco products and shall not be used for any personal attack on, or vilification of, any person (whether by name or business affiliation), company, or governmental agency, whether individually or collectively."

In other words, the settlement bars the kinds of ads that have been so successful in California and Massachusetts. The restriction isn't watertight—it only applies to the foundation created by the settlement, and states could use other funds to pay for anti-smoking campaigns. But that's not likely, given that the foundation is slated to get $25 million a year for education and media purposes. And many states have already made it clear that they intend to use the rest of the money to fill gaps in their budgets. New York City plans to use its share to clean up public schools, Los Angeles wants to repair its sidewalks, Louisiana will reduce the state debt, and Kentucky may use some of its money to help ailing tobacco farmers. Many of these states may find themselves running toothless anti-smoking campaigns—which is precisely what the tobacco industry wants. "If you want to see a recipe for failure, look at the settlement," says Stan Glantz.

That's why the states should take a second look at what really works when it comes to cutting back on smoking, and renegotiate or find a clear way around the restriction on attack ads. The federal lawsuit of the tobacco companies—which [President Bill] Clinton announced in his State of the Union speech—could provide another angle of attack. For starters, Clinton and the state attorneys general could point out that one of the stated purposes of the anti-smoking foundation created by November's settlement is to figure out which ads work best, regardless of their content. If attacking the industry proves consistently to be the best way to cut teen smoking rates, then there's no reason not to do it.

But most of all, we need to find new ways to make the truth about smoking come alive—and that means bringing the best minds on Madison Avenue to bear on the problem. It shouldn't be so hard: This is the generation reared on Monty Python, Wacky Packs, and *Mad* and *Spin* magazines. If we can make cigarettes seem laughable, we just might provide an example for countries like China, where 70 percent of men smoke and one in three is projected to die of smoking-related diseases within the next few decades. After all, once you reach that point it's almost too late for laughter. As one Adbusters satire of the short-lived Dakota cigarette brand put it: "Dakota. Dacough. Dacancer. Dacoffin."

14

Teens Are Working to End Teen Smoking

Steph Smith

Steph Smith is a writer for Scholastic News.

In the wake of her grandfather's death from lung cancer, teenager Kristy Ordonez became an antismoking activist. She came to understand that the tobacco industry, in order to continue making a profit, would need to find customers to replace those who died, as her grandfather had; and those replacements were the teenagers targeted by tobacco ads. Kristy developed strategies to mobilize adults in local government to work to make their community healthier by way of smoking restrictions.

Kristy Ordonez remembers her grandfather using an oxygen machine at home because he couldn't breathe on his own. Years of smoking cigarettes had robbed his body of the basic act of opening his mouth and taking in air. It wasn't long before he died of lung cancer.

What happened to her grandfather saddened Kristy, a 15-year-old teen from Ardmore, Oklahoma. But it wasn't surprising. Her grandfather was a long-time smoker, and it's no secret that smoking can cause or contribute to cancer, emphysema, and heart disease—serious illnesses that can kill a person.

Steph Smith, "Taking on Tobacco: This Teen Is on a Mission to Get Tobacco Products—and Advertisements Promoting Them—Away from Kids," *Scholastic Choices,* vol. 23, November-December, 2007, pp. 20–24. Copyright © 2007 Scholastic Inc. Reproduced by permission of the publisher.

Teens as Targets

But what Kristy learned next did surprise her. A member of Students Working Against Tobacco (SWAT) came to her school and told students that 1,200 people die every day in the United States from tobacco-related illnesses. The SWAT person also said that tobacco companies target teens as customers for their products. This is an accusation that tobacco companies deny, but the American Lung Association reports that 90 percent of smokers begin smoking before they turn 21 years old.

As a teen, Kristy doesn't have the power to ban tobacco products from public places, but she figured out how to convince adults in her community to act.

Kristy was facing some startling information. "The companies target teens because they need replacement smokers for the 1,200 people who die every day," Kristy tells *Choices*. "I'm being targeted to replace them."

She decided to join SWAT, and for the past three years, she has led SWAT campaigns to make public places in her town smoke-free, limit youth access to tobacco-product ads, and educate the public about the dangers of tobacco use. "It's about creating a healthier world, starting with your own community," Kristy says.

Kristy in Action

Here's how Kristy set out to accomplish her goals:

- *She put on a public display.* With other SWAT members, Kristy placed 1,200 pairs of shoes in front of a local hospital to represent the number of people who die every day from tobacco use.

- *She got political.* As a teen, Kristy doesn't have the power to ban tobacco products from public places, but she figured out how to convince adults in her commu-

nity to act. Kristy wrote letters to her city commission-
ers and gave a presentation to the entire commission.
She told the commission that people smoking in public
places sends a message to teens that smoking is an acceptable and harmless habit.

- *She targeted a big event.* Rodeos are popular where
  Kristy lives, and a smokeless tobacco company sponsors
  one in Oklahoma. Smokeless (chewing) tobacco is
  proven to cause cancer. Kristy believes the message to
  young people is clear.

"If they want to be cowboys, they have to have an imprint
in the shape of a chewing tobacco can in their back pocket,"
she says. Kristy's SWAT chapter protested against the chewing-
tobacco company's sponsorship of the rodeo.

The results of Kristy's efforts were mixed. It's impossible
to know how many people saw the shoes outside the hospital
and decided to try to stop smoking or to attempt to convince
a smoker they know to stop lighting up. But Kristy believes
that even if only one person acted after seeing the display, the
effort was worth it.

Her letter-writing campaign and presentation to the city
commission led to more concrete results. The city of Ardmore
passed an ordinance that bans tobacco products in areas used
mostly by people younger than 18.

The smokeless-tobacco company is still sponsoring rodeos,
but the fight isn't over. Kristy recently was named Central Regional Youth Advocate of the year by the Campaign for
Tobacco-Free Kids. She now is working with that group to get
a bill passed in the U.S. Congress. The bill would ban the
placement of tobacco advertisements where a lot of kids would
see them. It would also ban all remaining tobacco-brand spon-
sorships of sports and entertainment events—such as the rodeo.

Organizations to Contact

The editors have compiled the following list of organizations concerned with the issues debated in this book. The descriptions are derived from materials provided by the organizations. All have publications or information available for interested readers. The list was compiled on the date of publication of the present volume; the information provided here may change. Be aware that many organizations take several weeks or longer to respond to inquiries, so allow as much time as possible.

American Cancer Society
250 Williams Street, NW, #4D, Atlanta, GA   30303
(800) ACS-2345
Web site: www.cancer.org

The American Cancer Society is a nationwide community-based voluntary health organization dedicated to eliminating cancer as a major health problem by preventing cancer, saving lives, and diminishing suffering from cancer, through research, education, advocacy, and service. A number of publications are available including reports, surveys, and position papers.

American Legacy Foundation
1724 Massachusetts Avenue, NW, Washington, DC   20036
(202) 454-5555
Web site: www.americanlegacy.org

Created in 1999 out of the landmark Master Settlement Agreement between the tobacco industry, 46 state governments, and five U.S. territories, the American Legacy Foundation works to encourage youth to reject tobacco use as a part of their lives and to assist and empower smokers of all ages to quit. Programs include Truth—a youth smoking prevention campaign, and EX—a health program that seeks to communicate with current smokers in a nonthreatening manner, encouraging them to approach quitting in ways not considered in the past.

The foundation maintains a significant library of scientific reports, surveys, facts sheets, and publications related to tobacco use, its dangers, and cessation helps.

American Lung Association

61 Broadway, 6th Floor, New York, NY   10006
(800) LUNGUSA
Web site: www.lungusa.org

The mission of the American Lung Association is to prevent lung disease and promote lung health. Founded in 1904 to fight tuberculosis, the American Lung Association today fights lung disease in all its forms, with special emphasis on asthma, tobacco control, and environmental health. Reports, studies, position papers, and materials focused on smoking cessation are available.

Campaign for Tobacco-Free Kids

1400 Eye Street, Suite 1200, Washington, DC   20005
(202) 296-5469 (phone) • fax: (202) 296-5427
Web site: www.tobaccofreekids.org

The Campaign for Tobacco-Free Kids seeks to reduce tobacco use and its devastating consequences in the United States and around the world. By changing public attitudes and public policies on tobacco, the group aims to prevent children from smoking, help smokers quit, and protect everyone from secondhand smoke. Publications include press releases, facts sheets, and reports.

Cato Institute

1000 Massachusetts Avenue, NW
Washington, DC   20001-5403
(202) 842-0200
Web site: www.cato.org

The Cato Institute is a libertarian public-policy research foundation dedicated to limiting the control of government and protecting individual liberty. Its quarterly magazine *Regulation* has published articles and letters questioning the accuracy of U.S. Environmental Protection Agency studies on the dangers of secondhand smoke. The *Cato Journal* is published by the institute three times a year, and policy analysis papers are published periodically. Online resources and articles are continually updated.

FORCES International (Fight Ordinances and Restrictions to Control and Eliminate Smoking)

P.O. Box 533, Sutton, WV   26601
(304) 765-5394
e-mail: info@forces.org
Web site: www.forces.org

FORCES fights smoking ordinances and restrictions designed to eventually eliminate smoking, and it works to increase public awareness of smoking-related legislation. It opposes any state or local ordinance it feels is not fair to those who choose to smoke. Although FORCES does not advocate smoking, it asserts that an individual has the right to choose to smoke and that smokers should be accommodated where and when possible. The FORCES Web site contains a library of articles, online books, reviews, and out-of-print books, as well as recommended publications on a large number of subjects, including smokers' rights.

ImpacTeen

National Program Office, Chicago, IL   60608
(312) 413-0475 • fax: (312) 355-2801
e-mail: impacteen@uic.edu
Web site: www.impacteen.org

ImpacTeen is an interdisciplinary partnership of health experts with specialties in such areas as economics, etiology, epidemiology, law, political science, public policy, psychology, and sociology. The project, part of the Robert Wood Johnson Foundation's Bridging the Gap research initiative, focuses on economic, environmental, and policy influences on youth substance use, obesity, and physical activity. Materials available through impacTeen include research papers, presentations, policy briefs, reports, and other data related to smoking and youth.

New York City CLASH (Citizens Lobby Against Smoker Harassment)

P.O. Box 1036, Brooklyn, NY   11234
(917) 888-9317
e-mail: nycclash@nycclash.com
Web site: www.nycclash.com

CLASH seeks to end discrimination against smokers and to expose the deceptions put forward by the antismoking lobbies. To that end, CLASH maintains an online library of articles, papers, and essays on antismoking efforts throughout the years, as well as studies that question and contradict the scientific literature on the dangers of smoking.

National Institute on Drug Abuse (NIDA)

National Institutes of Health, Bethesda, MD   20892-9561
(301) 443-1124
Web site: www.nida.nih.gov

NIDA, a federal scientific research institute, is the largest supporter of the world's research on drug abuse and addiction. NIDA-funded scientific research addresses fundamental and essential questions about drug abuse, including tracking emerging drug-use trends, understanding how drugs work in the brain and body, developing and testing new drug treatment and prevention approaches, and disseminating findings to the general public and special populations. NIDA maintains a library of materials regarding smoking and other addictive substances geared toward youth, parents and educators, doctors and other health professionals, as well as researchers.

Tobacco Documents Online
Web site: www.tobaccodocuments.org

Tobacco Documents Online (TDO) is a search engine for all documents held by the tobacco industry regarding tobacco use and its effects on health. As part of the Master Settlement Agreement between states and tobacco companies, the industry was required to make the documents used during the trials available. The companies posted the documents on their Web sites, but searching required going to several different sites, each with a different interface. Through TDO, document descriptions have been standardized to allow uniform search and retrieval. The site offers searching across all the companies, access to high-quality images, and the ability to collect and annotate documents.

Bibliography

Books

George Latimer Apperson
The Social History of Smoking. Charleston, SC: BiblioBazaar, 2007.

Nazan Bayram, J.H. Owing, Alfredo Cheetah, Raffaele D'Ippolito
Smoking and Health: New Research. Hauppague, NY: Nova, 2005.

Richard J. Bonnie, Kathleen R. Stratton, Robert B. Wallace
Ending the Tobacco Problem: A Blueprint for the Nation. Washington, DC: National Academies Press, 2007.

David A. Brizer
Quitting Smoking for Dummies. Hoboken, NJ: Wiley, 2003.

Michael Dean
Empty Cribs: The Impact of Smoking on Child Health. Frederick, MD: Arts and Sciences, 2007.

Joan Esherick
Clearing the Haze: A Teen's Guide to Smoking-Related Health Issues. Broomall, PA: Mason Crest, 2004.

Calvin B. Fong
Smoking and Health Research Frontiers. Hauppague, NY: Nova, 2006.

Iain Gately
La Diva Nicotina: The Story of How Tobacco Seduced the World. New York: Simon and Schuster, 2002.

Sander L. Gilman and Xun Zhou — *Smoke: A Global History of Smoking.* London: Reaktion Books, 2004.

Margaret O. Hyde and John F. Setaro — *Smoking 101: An Overview for Teens.* Breckenridge, CO: Twenty-First Century Books, 2005.

J.H. Owing — *Trends in Smoking and Health Research.* Hauppague, NY: Nova, 2005.

Roddey Reid — *Globalizing Tobacco Control: Anti-Smoking Campaigns in California, France, and Japan.* Bloomington: Indiana University Press, 2005.

Frank A. Sloan et al. — *The Price of Smoking.* Boston: The MIT Press, 2006.

Frank A. Sloan, V. Kerry Smith, and Donald H. Taylor — *The Smoking Puzzle: Information, Risk Perception, and Choice.* Cambridge, MA: Harvard University Press, 2003.

Paul Slovic — *Smoking: Risk, Perception, and Policy.* Thousand Oaks, CA: Sage, 2001.

Penny Tinkler — *Smoke Signals: Women, Smoking and Visual Culture in Britain.* Oxford, UK: Berg, 2006

Periodicals

Siri Agrell — "Girls Get the Message," *Globe and Mail (Canada)*, July 10, 2007.

Lori Aratani — "Catching Up to the Boys, in the Good and the Bad," *Washington Post*, February 10, 2008.

Madeleine Brindley and Tomos Livingstone
"Pre-teens Who Date 'at Least Twice as Likely' to Turn into Smokers," *Western Mail*, December 1, 2006.

Elizabeth Cooney
"Eateries' Smoking Ban Is Dissuading Teens," *Boston Globe*, May 6, 2008.

Randy Dotinga
"A Link Between Teen Smoking and Movies?" *Christian Science Monitor*, November 22, 2005.

Evan R. Goldstein
"Smoking in the Movies," *Chronicle of Higher Education*, June 13, 2007.

Joseph Hall
"Doctors Push Smoking Ban in Cars with Kids," *Toronto Star*, February 15, 2008.

Theresa Howard
"Teens Actually Like Being Told Why Smoking's Dumb," *USA Today*, May 3, 2004.

Simon Jenkins
"Next the Anti-smoking Guardianistas Will Be Coming for Dogs and Cats," *Guardian (London)*, July 6, 2007.

Alok Jha
"Just One Cigarette in Childhood Can Lead to Later Addiction, Says Study," *Guardian (London)*, May 25, 2006.

Sharon Lem
"Teen Smokers Fall Short; Boys Won't Grow, Girls Won't Lose Weight," *Toronto Sun*, March 25, 2008.

Stephen Parnell "How I Doubled Our Smoking Quitters Using Reception Staff," *Pulse*, October 26, 2006.

Public Health Institute "There Is No Constitutional Right to Smoke," February 2004. http://www.phi.org/pdf-library/talc-memo-0051.pdf.

Anthony Ramirez "Teens in the City Smoke Less, Study Finds," *New York Times*, January 3, 2008.

Marisa Schultz, Amy Lee, and Eric Lacy "Workers Fume as Firms Ban Smoking at Home," *Detroit News*, January 27, 2005.

Judy Siegel-Itzkovich "Doctors Know About Lifestyle Counselling but Rarely Offer It," *Jerusalem Post*, March 18, 2007.

Carley Weeks "Teens Turning on to Flavoured Cigarellos," *Globe and Mail (Canada)*, June 24, 2008.

Index

A

Abel, Katy, 43

Academy Awards, 8

Acetylene, 60

ACS (American Cancer Society), 66, 80, 81, 93

Action on Smoking and Health, 40

Addiction, 35, 61, 62

Advertising, anti-smoking, 17, 62, 64–67, 81–82, 85

    See also Tobacco advertising

Aerosols, 19–20, 23

African-American teens, 58

Akwesasne reserve (Mohawk Nation Territory), 50, 51, 54

Altria Group, 18

AM PM retail stores, 27

American Academy of Pediatrics, 61

American Cancer Society (ACS), 66, 80, 81, 93

American Legacy Foundation, 16, 45, 64–67, 70, 92–93

American Lung Association, 46, 81–83, 91, 94

American Lung Association of Pennsylvania, 69

American Medical Association, 7–8

American Spirit cigarettes, 82

Anchorman (film), 7

Anderson, Gillian, 59

Anti-smoking initiatives

    campaigns, 17, 44, 62, 64–67, 85–87

    community ordinances, 62, 82, 87, 92

    satire, 85–86

    in schools, 68–72

    Truth brand, 64–67, 87

    See also Advertising, anti-smoking

Ardmore (OK), 90, 92

Arsenic, 33, 60, 79

Asthma, 60

Atlanta (GA), 15–16

Attractiveness, 20, 46, 61

B

Backwoods cigars, 37, 39

Banzhaf, John III, 81

Barkley, Amy, 75

Battle, Jerry, 76

Beauvais, Dwayne, 54–55

Benzene, 60

Big Tobacco, 27, 30, 77

Billboards, 82

Black market cigarettes

    chemicals in, 52

    organized crime and, 49

    police actions against, 49–54

    sources of, 48–51, 54

    taxes and, 48, 49

    See also Cigarettes

Blais, Andre, 38–39

Blum, Alan, 84

Boston University School of Public Health, 58

Brain, 61

Brazao, Dale, 47

Brewer, Shannon, 59

Brody, Jane E., 10